METROPOLIS NOW!

Ramesh Kumar Biswas (ed.)

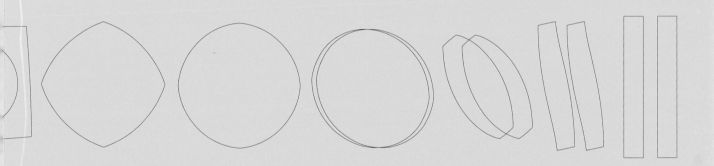

© 2000 Springer-Verlag/Wien
Printed in Austria

This work is subject to copyright.
All rights are reserved, whether the whole or part of the material is concerned, specifically those of translation, reprinting, re-use of illustrations, broadcasting, reproduction by photocopying machines or similar means, and storage in data banks.
Copyright for the essays remains with the respective authors, for the photographs with the photographers and for the video-symbol illustrations with Beatrix Bakondy.

Editor
Ramesh Kumar Biswas, biswas@gmx.net
www.rameshbiswas.com

Translations and proof reading
Ramesh Kumar Biswas, Chris Clouter, Nita Tandon, Susan Tapply

Graphic design and production
Beatrix Bakondy
Ramesh Kumar Biswas (Fusion 5 Multimedia)
Typeset in Frutiger

Printed on acid-free and chlorine-free bleached paper
Printed by Adolf Holzhausens Nfg., Vienna
Bound by Papyrus, Vienna
SPIN 10766593
CIP data applied for

ISBN 3-211-83496-6

METROPOLIS NOW!

Urban Cultures In Global Cities

Ramesh Kumar Biswas (ed.)

SpringerWienNewYork

A State Of Mind
Ramesh Kumar Biswas

A city is a state of mind. More than a mere collection of buildings and streets, it embodies the ideas of progress, of betterment, of success, of construction, but, as a matter of course, also their Siamese-twin mirror companions – failure, disappointment, tragedy, hopelessness and destruction. For all its false promises, the metropolis is as seductive as ever. One often hears that for the first time in history, more humans now live in urban centres than in rural areas. This banal statement ignores increasing anthropological, economic and archaeological indications that in many regions, the city came *before* the village, which itself was actually a by-product of certain urban forms of social organisation and consumption. It also overlooks the fact that the urban way of life is penetrating deeply into villages, whether they be in China or in Central Europe. The difference between city and land, however, is still marked. Those who live in cities have more in common with urban citizens in other parts of the world than with their fellow countrymen in villages. The enormous speed and the abilities that city dwellers must develop in order to process the ever-increasing amounts of information and stimuli that bombard them hourly are factors that contribute to the accelerated development of the brain. The city has long since taken over from food as the primary motor of human evolution. According to psychologist Stanton Newman and sociologist Susan

Lonsdale, we are now a new urban species, *homo urbanus*. And we are seeing the emergence of new, hybrid urban cultures.

Remember that even the gentle Aristotle considered only one possible way to deal with those who couldn't participate in or handle city life: "Off with their heads!", or its equivalent in Ancient Greek. It is not just the size of cities that is expanding, it is their aims, their possibilities, which are increasing dramatically with the wide availability of urban technologies. Far from decentralising or fragmenting societies, the new technologies are concentrating power and action in cities. More physical spaces are needed for the cyberworld, not less. Civil society is developing and connecting here, conflicts and cooperations are being shifted onto planes and dimensions that were unheard of before. "May you live in interesting times!", as the Chinese curse goes: for better or for worse, it is the 'citizen' who is creating, determining and steering the planet, its patterns of consumption and its cul-

tures. The metropolis is regaining the predominance that it lost to the nation-state in the nineteenth century. Today, it is not just economists who see the network of global cities and their cosmopolitan elite as the force that steers the development of nations.

This book is for the urban nomads of our times. People are travelling more than ever before. Statistics tell of a nation of four hundred and fifty million people who have undertaken international or intercontinental travel. While travel was once mainly aimed at escaping the city to various idylls of nature, city tourism is now increasing exponentially, just as is the number of people consecutively and temporarily resident in global centres for corporate, diplomatic, media, NGO or international public service employers. How are they to read or understand a strange city within a short period in order to be able to utilise and enjoy it? Although there has been a corresponding increase in the availability of travel guides, press features and

television programmes, these rarely scratch the surface. Even the better ones stop at describing the individual facets of a particular city – the mystery of why it is this way is generally left unexplored. And taxi drivers are *such* notoriously unreliable sources of information.

The portraits of cities here explore the deeper nature of cities, the milestones in their past that make them the way they are. They are not all-encompassing, but revealing. They look at people, how they use and change the city; at urban cultures that are not just cultural but economic and social. Each city is also used to exemplify at least one of the great themes of our time: globalisation, migration, civil society, environmental destruction, homelessness, the limits of planning and government, the information society, the consumer world, creativity, human relationships. It is no longer enough to just live in a city, to work or go home to sleep in it – one has to understand it and develop talents hitherto unknown to make best use of it.

This book is a reflection of the shift in emphasis that the social sciences have undergone, away from a 'scientific' listing of dates, individuals or ideologies, towards an intimate nearing to people, their private spheres and tendencies. This approach has seldom been applied to urban studies, which is usually strictly divided into the fields of planning, economics, geography, history or sociology. It is based on an

approach adopted by the Berlin periodical 'Stadtbauwelt', with which I have cooperated over the years. This book aims at a contemporary history of the metropolis; a subcutaneous analysis by academics who have not lost the capacity for awe, admiration and excitement. They are not just experts, but also *flaneurs*. Their critical approach to the cities they are writing about does not hide their obvious love for them. Sometimes objective outsiders – in the case of Singapore because local authors feared the consequences of an unfettered analysis – our observant visitors, who have often spent years in the respective cities, see things that residents may take for granted.

What do these cities have in common? Walls and gates. Berlin is by no means the only *polis* to have been divided by a wall and to have tried, with debatable success, to tear it down. Soweto and Johannesburg, Shanghai and Pudong, Marseille or Bombay all have walls of different materialities, separating people within the same space from each other. But cities also have gates that let in fresh breezes, new groups, ethnicities, ideas and cultural products, all of which undergo an unbelievable process of naturalisation and transformation. "*Stadtluft macht frei*" (city air makes you free), as an old German adage goes. Music or architecture, food or clothes, slang or lifestyle – every global product emerges fused with specific local elements to mutate further before being re-exported. Despite common fears of globalisation, we are, more than ever, seeing the emergence of the city *with* qualities. Each of these places has managed to remain unique.

You may well ask why these cities were chosen. London and Tokyo are obvious choices, but why Soweto? Because it represents a new image of emerging cities that is going to replace our traditional picture of high-rise skylines, and because it starkly emphasises the role of politics in shaping urban form. Why Marseille? Because it exemplifies an old meeting place of cultures with very con-

temporary difficulties in dealing with multiculturality. And what of those not included? Paris, Beijing, Jakarta, Barcelona or Rome will appear in a subsequent volume; and as for New York, there are already so many Woody Allen films.

The choice is, to a degree, personal. I am impressed by cities with enormous problems which, like Baron Munchhausen, grab their own pigtails and attempt to pull themselves out of the mire. I am fascinated by centres of conflict between times, cultures, generations, classes, minorities and systems; by laboratories for living in the future. I wallow in streets full of humour and cruelty, I revel in the shimmering light and the heavy shadows, I enjoy the friendly warmth that comforts and the danger that keeps me going. The metropolis is a state of mind – each portrait tells you as much about the author as about the city itself.

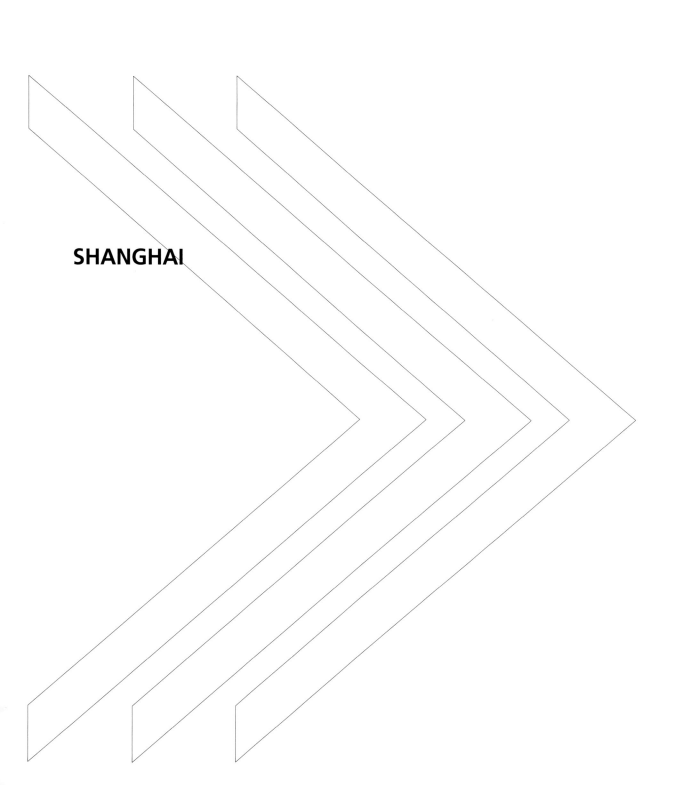

SHANGHAI

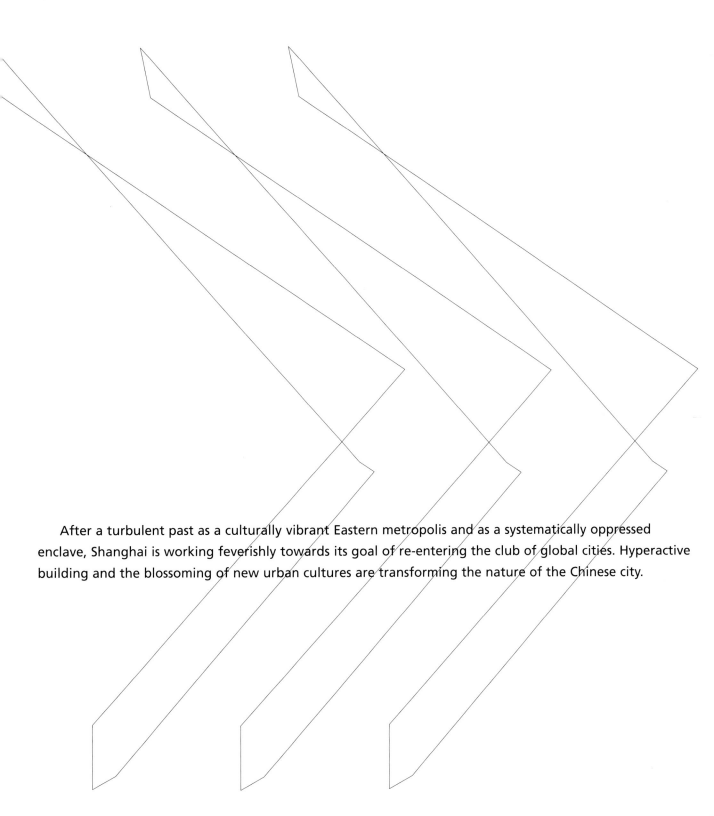

After a turbulent past as a culturally vibrant Eastern metropolis and as a systematically oppressed enclave, Shanghai is working feverishly towards its goal of re-entering the club of global cities. Hyperactive building and the blossoming of new urban cultures are transforming the nature of the Chinese city.

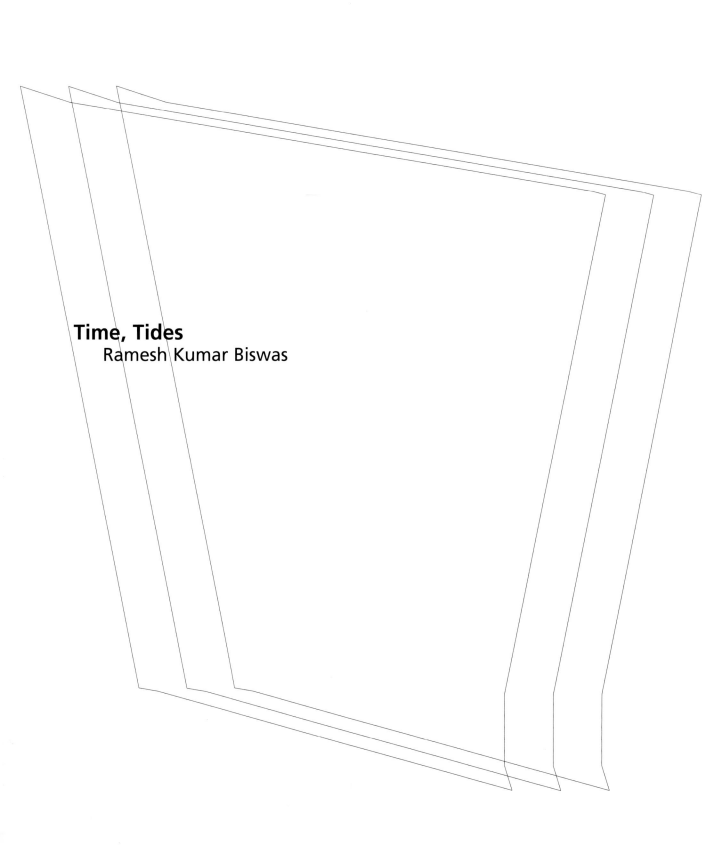

Time, Tides
Ramesh Kumar Biswas

Shanghainese live more in time than in space, even when space tends to vanish without warning and time sometimes acquires spatial gestalt. While Beijing can still be defined by its physical characteristics – static architectural mass fixed in space – Shanghai, on the contrary, is associated above all with time – fluidity, instability, transience, fantasy, phantasmagoria, intoxication, ecstasy, disillusionment. A kaleidoscope, continually rotating. It would not do justice to this city to force it into the straitjacket of classical urbanisation of either the Western industrial world or the Third World. Shanghai is a special case in a special country. The critical point in the configuration of Shanghai is the instability of perceptible space. As the artist Yung Ho-Chang asks, "If space is no longer at work as the paramount urban infrastructure, does it mean that time, once minor order-giver, may do the job of organising events of the city all by itself?".

SHANGHAI

Shanghai is a city of passers-by. For a hundred years educated Chinese, hungry for action, streamed into the foreign concessions of Shanghai to escape the repressive rules and customs of the bureaucratic Confucian establishment. Its very name awakens associations with armed diplomats, tea-sipping matrons, striking workers, opium addicts, flirtatious beauties, revengeful Red Guards and starving beggars. Rebellious students and writers, businessmen and artists came to realise their potential in Shanghai. The successful commercial harbour, serving 800 000 km of waterways in South China, was transformed from 1919 to 1927 by foreign entrepreneurs, a new class of urban Chinese, and plentiful cheap rural labour escaping starvation into a dynamic industrial city, a pioneer in urban technologies and comforts. More than 40% of the nation's invested industrial capital, production and industrial workforce were based here. Capitalists from the Straits of Malacca or Central Europe, and Chinese from the hinterland enriched themselves in the foreign enclaves, where they shamelessly created privileges for themselves. At the same time they helped form an intellectually and culturally vibrant city with a lively film industry, courageous publishing houses, iconoclastic literature and radical political groups, among them the intellectual elite of the Communist Party. It had the decadence of Paris, the 'jazz' of New York, the audacity of Berlin. Future was set against tradition, the local against the international in a city full of grotesque superlatives – the City that Never Sleeps, the Paris of the Orient, the Swamp of Sin, the Whore of the East and so on – as the travel-guide *clichés* abounded even at the time. This cosmopolitan culture opened itself to ideas and lifestyles of a new society that strengthened as the old system sank into chaos and strife.

The elite and the workers alike came looking for more than work – they were looking for freedom from the old customs and a breath of the wide world outside. They were consumers of the new films and customers of the new shops. They paraded in audacious clothes before the cafes, the boutiques and the nightclubs in the Nanjing Road or the rue de Joffre. The men in natty Western suits. The women in *cheongsams*, modestly closed at the collar but slit both sides right up from the ankles to the hips. This dress, guaranteed to raise blood pressure, was a symbol of the sensuousness of the city and its collision with the China of old.

Passports were not required for entry. Desperados, opportunists and refugees: white Russians, persecuted Jews, Scottish bankers, liberal Japanese and a few common gangsters landed from the steamers looking for the quick dollar and the quicky, Calvinist missionaries and American cowboys added to the explosive mix. Their naked greed was given a respectable facade that still graces miles of serious grey granite on the Bund: Jardine Matheson & Co., Butterfield and Swire, Chartered Bank, Hong Kong and Shanghai Banking Corporation.

Behind it the dealers, financiers and bureaucrats exploited local workers economically and sexually with a ruthlessness that would not have been possible at home. Stunning beauties with price tags drove around in rickshaws with colourful lamps in the Nanjing Road, past strolling men looking for either plain and simple sex, or the other varieties of it. Shanghai was represented in Chinese film and literature as the seductive woman, femininity itself, while Beijing was still the buttoned-up bureaucrat. "It's stupid not to look for women here! What does Shanghai have in greater surplus than women? Where does one find women easier to seduce?" cries a jubilant character in Shi Tuo's major work 'Marriage'.

Speculation and prostitution flourished as two shady institutions, the stock market and the bordel, mingled. The secret societies dominated the Chinese quarter. And while champagne was sipped in the clubs and opium smoked in the drug holes, dead bodies were picked up from the streets and carried away silently in hand carts by municipal employees every day at the crack of dawn.

It was this decadent, egoistic heartlessness of Shanghai that the Communists used to justify their systematic humiliation and decimation of Shanghai's culture for 30 long years after the Revolution. They marched in peacefully enough, put an end to the worst conditions, and then began to fundamentally change the place. Brutal anti-capitalist and anti-foreigner campaigns were focussed on the hated (though secretly envied) cosmopolites of Shanghai. Street committees made up of sanctimonious rural cadres publicly executed 'blackmarketeers', guarded every aspect of daily life, set up files on every citizen and painted the colourful city effectively grey. All that was fine and elegant was eradicated with such a remarkable thoroughness, that it was nothing less than a kind of exorcism. The extravagant and unique street life was eliminated without regard for the individuals involved, as one can now read in numerous Chinese memoirs. Alternative entertainment was provided: businessmen were forced to denounce each other at public meetings, to be subsequently relieved of their property and deported to work camps. Night clubs, publishing houses, bookshops and boutiques were closed down. "Shanghai is an unproductive city, a parasitic city, a criminal city, a pleasure city, a refugee city, a paradise for adventurers", declared the Party organ Economic Weekly in August 1949, in an article probably not intended for the promotion of tourism. In the following years over a million academics, technicians and specialist workers were sent to other cities; complete factories were dismantled and rebuilt in northern China.

The Opera was shut down and the famous Shanghai Club with its forty-metre long bar was closed, to henceforth secretly serve as Mao's Shanghai residence, as his personal physician recently revealed.

The city's treasury was confiscated by the Centre to support the national Chinese budget for decades. This booming economy was reduced to the worst regional performance within China in 1985, comparable only to Tibet. During the 1980s, over half of the industrial machinery in use was installed in the 1930s, and innovation, that is, "the transfer of research to production, never went beyond the stage of the gift, the prototype or the exhibition piece" as economist Detlef Rehn notes. It was only after the reforms and the rise of Shanghainese to important positions in the Beijing hierarchy that the city was once again allowed to utilise at least part of its income to improve infrastructure and housing. After Deng triumphed ideologically over his rivals, individual initiative and success were once again encouraged. Millions of academics and bureaucrats have profited from the *xiahai* (leap into the sea) campaign – Shanghai slang for starting a private enterprise. The average resident's income has increased manifold to €1980, while economic growth rates have overtaken even the high Chinese average. As a reaction against the indoctrinated simplicity of past decades, many of the nouveau riche are conspicuously showing off their wealth. They parade, without false modesty, in the newly reopened Shanghai Club. The streets look like a trade fair of limousines, with young couples flaunting Western fashion, jewellery, brand names and the ultimate status symbol, that only the really rich can afford – a second child.

The city is going through violent and confusing transformations. Time has turned it inside out. In breathless and purposeful hyperactivity a new form is emerging that is radically changing the image of the Chinese city. The old quarters of row houses, called '*lilongs*', romantic and close-knit, but overcrowded and under-serviced, are being feverishly documented by various architects and historians, but are disappearing without widespread protest, apart from sadness about the disintegration of neighbourhoods. The physical and psychological perception of the city has been shifted by the raised urban motorways being slashed through, or, partly, over Shanghai. The local, ground level view of individuals in a city at their daily activities was first supplemented by the topographic outlook, the global birds-eye view, provided initially by movies and skyscrapers and now by high-level urban motorways. What appears from a distance to be hairy snakes are Neo-Brutalist constructions, prettified by weeping willows, that offer the citizen a thoroughly fascinating experience. One usually drives at fifth-storey level. I once counted 14 storeys under us in the building next to the motorway we were driving on. The urban *gestalt* at this level is defined by skyscrapers, while the low-rise, older quarters appear from above to be nothing more than potential construction sites. A convenient shift in perception that prepares a favourable atmosphere for the developer. The impressive, paralysing panoramic view is "an optical artefact, a projection, a spectacle, a theoretical simulacrum full of misunderstandings" (Michel de Certeau). It is the view lower down that is more dependable, revealing. Walking through everyday life the labyrinth sucks you in, the enigma looking for a solution, the complex connections between apparently fragmented places. This is the mysterium, here lies the fascination of the Chinese city, this is where the urban cultures assert themselves.

Let us not forget that China has 3000 years of sophisticated city building behind it. It is, besides India, the land with the longest uninterrupted process of urbanisation. A certain conceptual image of the city existed as a cosmological-magical figure before cities in the Shang and Zhou Dynasties in the 2nd and 1st millenia BCE, though ritual city-like structures were built as early as the 3rd millenium BCE. Chang'an and Suzhou were the world's most populous cities in the 8th century CE. Major trading cities of the Song Dynasty (960–1279 CE), Hanghzhou and Kaifeng had one and a half million citizens each, at a time when the biggest European city did not even house fifty thousand souls. But it was not the mere masses that made the Chinese city, it was also urban design – the great city centres, the grandiose palaces, the refined gardens. All the preconditions for a lively urban culture existed, but the potential for manifold urban cultures or economic activities was not entirely fulfilled in Chinese cities, with the exception of the five 'open' cities like Kaifeng on the Silk Road.

At the same time, the important Italian, Persian, Arabic, Hanseatic and Indian cities were cauldrons bubbling with external influences, trade, political activity, free intellectual institutions, struggles for autonomy from rural aristocracy and from central power structures – all of which led to independent, identifiable urban cultures. In a nutshell: it was the opening of these latter cities inwards and outwards that enabled the breakthrough, so that one could talk of these cities metaphorically as gates.

Walls, not gates, were the central concept of the Chinese city, so central that the traditional symbol 'cheng' stood for both city and wall. The majority of the urban population was concentrated *intra muros*, symbols of power and control, part of a great imperial plan. An urban settlement without a wall was not considered a proper city. Beijing was a wall, a *glacis* against invading hordes, long before it became a city. During the monarchies, most Chinese cities were primarily highly controlled administrative centres, where bureaucrats and soldiers dominated. Meetings were forbidden, and the evening curfew alone guaranteed that the normal population could not develop any other activities in the city outside their work. How could even the germ of a diverse and colourful urban culture develop under such conditions? Of course, the highly educated and bored mandarins in provincial cities enjoyed and developed an upper-class culture in the course of long evening *soirées* in private homes, tea houses and courtesan quarters. Painting, music, calligraphy and poetry attained their heights, refined by primarily male groups of land-owning and hence rural-minded bureaucrats. Naturally, the concept of culture encompasses high culture as well as everyday culture, which are bound together if only because the craftsmanship of the latter enables the practice of the former. However, a look at the larger picture shows the gaping cleft between the two.

Order and quiet dominated the public arena and suffocated any spontaneous street life that came into being.

Even when the walls finally offered no protection against the invading Mongolian, Manchurian, European and Japanese conquerors, for centuries they defined the centralist power relationships and the petrified defences of Beijing against any change, against anything new, against foreigners and their ideas. Only Shanghai and Hong Kong, where tempo determined growth more than physical structures, escaped this narrowness due to their special position. Besides walls, it is other elements like markets and public squares, or the lack of them, that determine urban culture. Even under the restrictive regulations, some street life managed to develop until it was nipped in the bud again in the 1950s. Itinerant traders, street stalls and food markets disappeared after the Revolution to be replaced by huge ration halls with all the charm of concrete bunkers, eliminating the last bit of colour from the streets. Since the free exchange of opinion demands its own public urban space, the authorities decided for the sake of convenience to dispense with both. A professor of planning from Shenzen expressed it unusually directly: "squares like the agora in ancient Greece were brought into being by a democracy, however flawed. We in China have never had a democracy, and as a consequence, hardly any public piazzas. What does exist are corridors for troops to march up and down, like Tiananmen; avenues for imperial processions; and heavenly axes."

The concept of the urban resident who acted on his own motivation did not exist historically, as the film critic Zhang Ying Jin notes. The Greek or Italian 'citizen' with specific rights and duties was unknown here. Besides this, the predominantly rural nature and mind-set of Chinese society (the urban populace has been stable for centuries until recently at around 20% of the total population) hindered the development of urban culture. Cities did not have a legal status that differed from that of rural areas. This attitude is only just changing due to the recent intensive urbanisation of rural life, which itself will have an enormous impact on urban culture in cities, as migrants would now tend to adopt urban lifestyles rather than transfer their familiar rural way to urban ghettos.

Bureaucrats from Beijing are only moderately reformist. They distrust the liberalism, the openness, the scepticism and the lust for life of the southern coastal cities. While Beijing could still be described by terms like tradition and permanence, Shanghai is a *gudao*, a 'lonely island', isolated from tradition, cut off from China's history, floating in a sea of modernity, change and insecurity.

The recent transformations have been accelerated by the relaxation of the system. The *danwei* – communal factories, walled and guarded areas that formerly occupied entire urban quarters – have been transformed by part-privatisation into public spaces. Even the external walls of these *danwei*, earlier accessible only to their employees, have being punctured by little shops, holes in the wall that allow the emergence of specific local cultures. This process is transforming Shanghai just as much as the construction of skyscrapers. The post-political city has been emerging since the Eighties. It is a pleasure to walk around and absorb the varied, hectic activities. People are out in the streets and parks again, waltzing or *tai-chi*-boxing, comparing their caged singing birds, yelling into their mobile phones, having an intimate moment with a lover away from their crowded flats. The average worker is no longer compelled to enjoy hours of uplifting 'political education' classes after work in his factory. The time gained is now spent with friends, neighbours and relatives, which has in turn led to the opening of local clubs and food stalls; or spent in consumer activities, encouraging numerous services, shops and restaurants to sprout up everywhere. But entire streets full of dozens of little 'hairdresser's salons' that are open till three in the morning? It looks as if the decadent Shanghai of old is back with a vengeance.

The new Shanghai, however, as much symbol as physical city, is appearing on the far bank of the river. Facing the majestic Bund, now a popular promenade, is one of the biggest urban experiments in history: the new city of Pudong, literally, "east of the (Huang)pu" river. It took a turbulent 200 years for the Western world to make the transition from a rural subsistence economy to a society that lives in flats, shops in supermarkets and gobbles fast food. In Pudong this process is supposed to take only 30 years. To this end a quarter of all the cranes in the world are rotating here on 22 000 building sites. Mao Zedong's world view, that man flourishes best when raised as an organically grown, free-range, ground-level farming product, has been turned on its head: from now on he is expected, perched at a height of 60 metres, to stare at other towers directly in front of his nose.

The powers-that-be declared at the beginning of the 'Four Modernizations' campaign in the early 1980s that the municipal area of Shanghai was far too small to fulfil its future role as a world city. And so Shanghai was expanded as it has been often in the past. Hitherto rural Pudong was divided into five planning zones: the industrial area, the free trade zone, the telecommunications zone, the harbour and above all Lujiazui, directly across the river from the Bund, designated the future Chinese centre of finance and services. When the Pudong New Area was officially declared into existence in 1990, this future global financial node had a largely rural population of 1.3 million people, with only 20 000 telephone numbers and about 30 times as many chickens.

In China, statistics are supplied solely by the government. They serve primarily as a tool for the retention of power and inner stability, secondarily as a kind of work therapy for the many State-run publishing houses and institutes. I didn't know whether to be amused or amazed when I learned at Tongji University that there are "closed" and "public" urban development plans for Pudong. Though it is clear to anybody that it is impossible to direct the development of a city with different versions of plans, the main purpose of manipulated information, or even just the withholding of information, is nothing but effective control over millions of people. Of course, this is nothing new in Shanghai. A look at earlier English and Chinese maps of the city show that each of them conveniently ignored the existence of the other. The international maps whited out the Chinese city or depicted it as an integral part of the foreign settlements, whereas the Chinese maps emphasised the magistrate as the centre of a Chinese city untainted by foreign presence. As the sinologist Catherine Yeh records, there was a whole range of maps for military, business, administration or leisure purposes, all propaganda tools to impress, legitimise, heighten or lower resistance, which reflected the strategies of the two communities and their confrontations. In his book 'How To Lie With Maps', Mark Monmonier notes that "a single map is but one of an indefinitely large number of maps that might be produced for the same situation or from the same data". The Chinese authorities seem to have taken this philosophy to heart. In any case, the official figure first given for the area of Pudong was 350 square kilometres, with large blank areas on the plan. An independent computer-aided planimeter programme calculated the actual area as 518 square kilometres, but could not explain the reason for the difference, which has since been officially corrected without further explanation. On another plane, the different maps of Shanghai could be seen as an unintentional metaphor for the different realities and societies that overlap here, making it the multi-layered cosmopolitan metropolis it is.

In three phases, of which the second is nearing completion, 177 sq. km of this area are to be transformed into a fully developed urban zone, bigger even than present-day Shanghai, Singapore or London. The five zones are to be connected with an plethora of motorways and infrastructure, industry is supposed to be "clean" and supported by scientific and educational districts. The underground lines, the new 24-hour airport, various residential, business, and leisure centres are being opened according to plan, though the plan is not forthcoming about details of the proposed "natural and ecological environment". (As James sees it the *I-Ching* declares the cosmic principle of organisation at all levels is coterminous with and inseparable from *chhi*, or matter-energy. In other words, it's the thought that counts). The city government does not count on the powers of the free market and is hence playing an active and regulatory role. According to the declaration, financing is to be shared between the central government, the city of Shanghai, foreign investors, and the unsuspecting "Chinese people". Although information about investment structures is full of gaps, what can be said with certainty is that Beijing has invested € 575 million annually in Pudong since 1990, either directly or through loans. Beyond that, special legal arrangements have been made for business transactions and currency movements, access for foreigners, permits, customs, taxes and functional zoning plans. A report by the international real estate agents Jones Lang Wooton notes that, contrary to general assumptions, no more than a fifth of the high-rise buildings in Pudong have been built with foreign money, most of which again is 'ethnic Chinese' investment from Hong Kong, Singapore, Malaysia and Taiwan. The vast majority consists of direct investments of regional governments or State-owned firms with loans from State-owned banks which do not have to bother much about commercial returns. This relationship is mirrored in building projects – Zheng Shiling, Vice President of Tongji University, estimates that of the 2000 new high-rise buildings completed so far, only 80 were planned abroad. The towers are kitsch to a fault. The Oriental Pearl Tower is a built version of a Taoist contemplative about seven pearls – visible proof that Chinese poems do not easily lend themselves to translation into TV towers. Once you penetrate the expensive facades, you are bound to be disappointed by the shabby interiors (a case of "saving face" translated into architecture?). Of course, many of the buildings are faithful copies of towers in other world cities. If Celebration is the Disney town, Pudong is the Xerox city; if romance is the spirit of Paris, *déjà vu* is the Pudong feeling.

As much else in Shanghai, even visionary plans for Pudong are not new. Since it was not under international rule, the Chinese attempted to set up an administration and infrastructure here that would compete with those of Shanghai. Even nationalists in Shanghai differed from their collegues in the rest of China, in that they were forward-looking modernisers, not backward-looking Confucian scholars. In April 1921 the Nationalist leader Sun Yatsen declared his plan for the development of the big harbour in Pudong as a key project of national reconstruction. His compatriots who had studied abroad or in the new local universities saw democracy, technology and pragmatism as a cure for China's ills. Of course, economic considerations dominated even then – land prices in Pudong were six thousand times lower than in Shanghai itself. One could thus avoid expensive renovations to the old harbour and political confrontation with the imperialists and the population of Shanghai. The radical plan to divert and straighten the Huangpu river was obviously inspired by the then recently completed Panama Canal.

The river, as we can see for ourselves, is still flowing its old crooked way. Sun Yatsen's plan, discarded upon his death in 1925, is seen by the present administration as an "impractical but worthy" research basis for the urban planning of Pudong. The Guomindang fled to Taiwan, but even the victorious Communists were unable to achieve much until Deng's reforms in 1978 and the 1990 declaration of Pudong New Area as a "socialist, modern region", or whatever that was decoded as. Today Sun Yatsen is actually praised for his vision – miracles occur even in atheistic societies.

But, as with all miracles, caution is highly recommended. The enormous amount of over-priced, monofunctional development, the promoters of which are variously multinational companies, the Red Army or even the Folk Dance Society, represent not only an aesthetically disappointing mayonnaise resulting from conflicting interests, but also a questionable change in the quality of life for the residents. The massive displacement of rural communities and their transfer to disparate, incomplete housing estates centrifuges social structures. But even the new over-dimensioned open spaces or avenues, especially in the central three square km of Lujiazui, seem to negate the reality of local society. They are meant for business-suited men descending from black limousines, but there is little space for cyclists, small repair shops, food stores, markets, protected street corners, niches for the aged, or intimate structures. Both these worlds could easily have been accommodated in this huge project. Even more unwise is the widespread use of climatically inappropriate building types, foremost among them being the inefficient American-type high-rise with a fridge on top of it. Energy production from outdated coal-burning plants has already ruined the air and the water, and one may well ask whether these wastefully conceived high-rises are going to be shut down come the next energy crisis. China's recent entry into the WTO is going to make cars considerably cheaper and lungs considerably blacker.

The present Pudong project shares with its predecessors the assumption that national economic development and urbanisation are intricately connected, and that the great cities are the only arena where economic development takes place, even when the price to be paid is high in terms of pollution, unemployment and social tensions. Pudong is far more than an attempted diversion from Tiananmen, as some cynics have it. Deng Xiaoping challenged his comrades to see the development of Pudong as a chance to "free our way of thought" and to "abolish our straitjackets". Terminally ill, he travelled in 1992 to Shanghai to deposit his astonishing message personally. Whereas the Beijing leadership is still thinking about a possible cohabitation of a one-party state with a free economic sector – after all it did work quite well for a while in South Korea, Indonesia or Taiwan – Shanghai itself goes much further. Pudong is seen here as the last chance to create a modern Shanghai, to fully exploit the enormous human potential available, to disempower the fossilised bureaucracy and, in the long run, to uncouple itself from the rest of China. All these plans and projects raise more questions than they answer. Pudong, unlike ancient Rome, has been built in a day. But the first doubting voices are beginning to be heard.

There is no denying the massive volume of building, the astronomical profits and the impressive energy on show. Shanghai has successes galore: the rise in its number of its airline city links, volume of airfreight, number of foreign firms, sum of foreign investment, extent of the information highway network, banking operations and other classical economic indicators show an impressive improvement compared to Hong Kong, as urban analyst Saskia Sassen records. However crucial economic factors are to an understanding of a city, they are not the whole story. As has been noted, within China Shanghai serves once again as a node of crystallisation of numerous discourses and value systems: tradition versus modernity, individualism versus collectivism, prosperity versus modesty, bourgeoisie versus proletariat, the "right" way versus the expedient way, neo-colonialism versus nationalism. The central government views every success story in Shanghai with a mixture of pride and unease, as it rightly fears any major forthcoming political challenge to emerge from here. Their long and painful history has made a well-informed, widely networked and critical community of the Shanghainese. Products for mass cultural consumption, such as films, TV series, books, magazines, songs and plays, while not openly criticising the government, are slowly and subtly subverting the system more effectively than a frontal attack, sinologist Erich Pilz observes. Irony, exaggerated sensationalism and humour are being applied as popular counter-propaganda. Hybrid cultural forms are blooming again. The relative openness and transparency of recent years has led to a more balanced analysis of the Chinese city than to which Chinese experts themselves have been able to contribute objectively for the first time. Earlier romanticisations by "China hands" about the Chinese road to urbanisation are being seen in a new light.

What is undoubtedly striking about Chinese cities is that there is far less abject poverty, overcrowding or traffic congestion, far fewer rubbish heaps or slums than in Asian or African cities, and no one is starving on the streets, all of which one must acknowledge without a trace of sarcasm as great achievements. The different path urban development has taken here lies in China-specific factors: low birth rates in cities due to higher female employment and the single-child policy, the ideologically motivated depopulation of the cities during "back-to-the-land" campaigns in the Sixties, the de-investment in Shanghai, the system of temporary workers from the countryside, the strict urban resident registration laws and the low urban multiplicator effect of industrial production – all this led to 'under-urbanisation' as opposed to 'over-urbanisation' elsewhere. But China's future is now closely coupled with the urbanisation process in Asia (in fact some Chinese bemoan their cities becoming increasingly like other "Third-World cities") and the Asian economy is not as strong as it was when Shenzhen was built. As a slightly desperate Frankfurt banker put it, "The assumption that 1.2 billion mouths need electric toothbrushes and 2.4 billion armpits need deodorant sprays turned out to be a miscalculation". Just another in a series of classic misconceptions of China that have plagued the outside world for centuries. For all its fascination with the Western world, China is not going to give up its identity completely. While visiting someone in Shanghai, I noticed him setting up a mousetrap – not with cheese, but with a piece of cuttlefish marinated with a couple of drops of soy and decorated with a slice of pickled ginger.

Shanghai is seizing every opportunity that comes its way. The spread of telecommunications technology has altered the consciousness of urban dwellers more than anything else. In front of the TV screen, in the free space of the Web in simple cybercafes and in the universities, a new picture of the world, a new horizon is opening up for the younger generation. They are giving a specific local face to modernity and are simultaneously using the city as a portal through which they will project themselves into the outer world. They feel an increasing purpose to emerge from behind the protective mask of assumed cultural uniqueness and to meet the world and its curious citizens on its own terms. The critical question of the re-entry of Shanghai into the club of world cities is the question of internal and external migration. As one of the five open Chinese cities of the Treaty of Nanjing and as the fifth-largest city in the world in 1936, Shanghai profited enormously from the influence of all those who streamed there and created new hybrid cultures for a hundred years. However, the China that governs Shanghai is a monolithic state of 96% Han Chinese, traditionally convinced of their superiority over other peoples. In all of China today there are less than two hundred thousand foreigners, less than in restrictive Vienna alone. Shanghai would then have to be the first monoethnic and monocultural global city, a concept that is difficult to imagine or to realise today. Even Tokyo, though monoethnic, is pluricultural. World cities develop their own dynamics that are not easy to regulate, and Shanghai itself has experienced this before. The inner-Chinese migration could well be controlled for another few years through old methods of city residence permits. There exist secret agreements between the city and governments of surrounding regions that any slack in the building boom would lead to trains travelling in one direction, taking back construction workers to their home villages. Tickets to Shanghai would then not be available in the province. But how are Chinese cities going to survive when the present political possibilities for imposing such draconian controls no longer exist? And what are the consequences of foreign immigration that goes beyond a few tens of thousands of wealthy managers? It is difficult for the Chinese to imagine at the moment, but if Shanghai achieves even a few of its own goals, it could become very attractive for a Fillippino nurse, a Bangladeshi hotel worker, a Spanish cook, an unemployed doctor from Germany or a specialist carpenter from Indonesia. Which changes to its identity is it going to accept, which others are going to roll over it regardless?

All the enthusiasm and energy one feels in Shanghai cannot cover up some sobering thoughts, often voiced by residents themselves. The social exclusion of the local "floating population" of temporary workers is just another facet of the immigration problem. Other dangers lie in the polarisation of the job market, traffic congestion, lagging investment in infrastructure, loss of built heritage, monofunctional concentration, pollution, overcrowding, lifestyle gaps reflected either in gated or in dislocated communities, and unemployment (euphemistically known as *xiagang*, or "freedom from work"). To add to this is the increase in crime at various levels: several bureaucrats seem to have adopted a new post-communist pension plan, commonly known as corruption. The streets are not as safe as they used to be, and the reborn triads have joined hands with international syndicates on fertile fields. Its residents seemed to take all these new developments in their stride. Shanghai is slowly on its way, they say, after a turbulent life as a special case, to becoming a *normal* city, with all its attendant problems. At last.

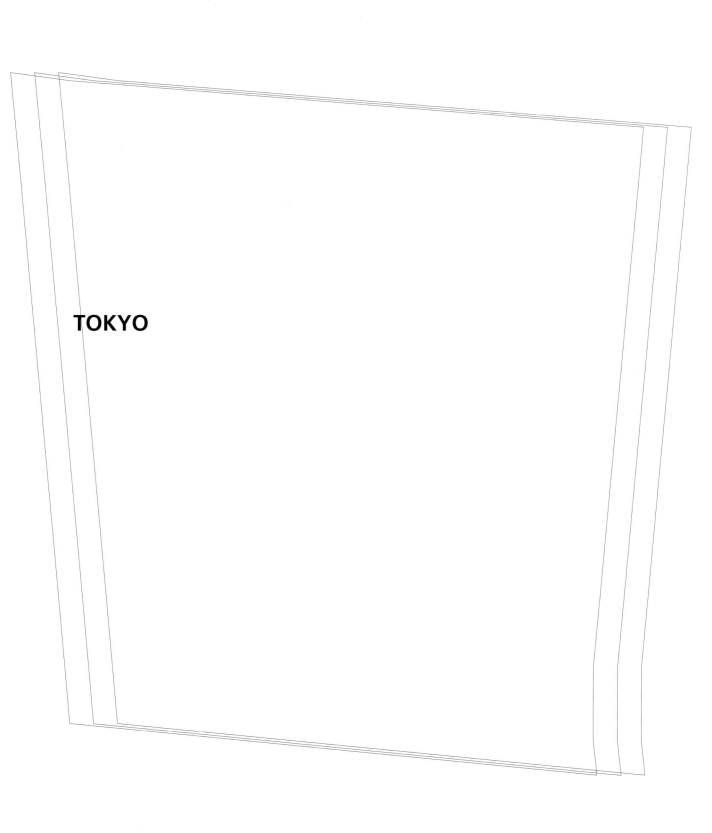

TOKYO

The pounding, chattering rhythms among towering high-rises or the quiet, clandestine alleys in village-like neighbourhoods characterise the contradictions of daily life in the fastest and richest city in the world. Tokyo is an experimental field where every urban trend appears for the first time, to be copied years later in other world cities.

Different With A Difference
Roman Cybriwsky

TOKYO

Forbidden to outsiders for 250 years, destroyed by an earthquake in 1923, carpet bombed in 1945, Tokyo is a city which never looks back and continues to write the future of cities everywhere. It now sits at the top of the world as one of its largest and most influential urban areas, and looks forward with confidence to an even greater role in the twenty-first century. It is, arguably, the economic capital of the Pacific Rim, and its time in history is the Pacific Century, which is either already in full swing or just about to begin, depending on how you define the term. Just as London was on the rise as the world's dominant city in 1800, and New York was ascendant in 1900, it is Tokyo that strives for primacy at the millennium marker.

Tokyo's National Capital Region, defined as Metropolitan *Tōkyō-to* plus four surrounding prefectures, is by far the world's largest, exceeding second-placed New York by some 18 million souls. *Tōkyō-to* itself, the city's formal geographical unit, totals 12.7 million. Even more important than population is the city's dominant role in the world economy. According to Saskia Sassen, Tokyo is a global leader in terms of lending, stocks, mega-banks, securities and corporate headquarters, and ranks, along with New York and London, as one of three principal 'command centres' of the international economy. The Tokai Bank has calculated that the city is now so important that Western economies would collapse if Tokyo were to be devastated again by one of its periodic great earthquakes; as Japanese companies liquidate their assets abroad to finance urban reconstruction.

In addition to being enormously important, Tokyo is also incredibly interesting. To be there is to experience one of the most dynamic and changeable cities of all time. It is also to feel a city that is uncommonly rich in traditions. This is a duality that represents the essence of Tokyo, and makes it so challenging to understand and fun to know. At one instant, one thinks of Tokyo as a thoroughly modern, international place that belongs clearly at the forefront of the greatest cities. It is superbly style-conscious, is attuned to and often creates the latest trends, and is a mecca for culture. It is thoroughly delightful for its many spectacular examples of contemporary architecture, its wonderful department stores and many other attractions. But in the next instant, there is a change of scene and something happens to present Tokyo as a small town rather than a giant city, and as a place that is forever tied to the past rather than at the cutting edge of the future. So too, one is reminded again and again that the city has been shaped very much by forces that are distinctively Japanese and very alien to the habits of other realms. Yet, in these instances too, Tokyo displays uncommon greatness. As a result it is hard not to love the city and harder still to avoid becoming immersed in its myriad details.

No matter where I went in the city over the years, a special kind of urban differentness would reveal itself and draw me closer. Paul Waley, historian, writes, "Tokyo is different with a difference". I tend to concentrate on the look of the city – a useable record of urban society – on landscapes or cityscapes that reveal so much about the people who shaped them. However, as interesting as it is to walk the city, Tokyo poses special problems in this regard, as tragic disasters have erased most of the historic fabric, and much of what exists is designed primarily for show and does not necessarily represent the true nature or innermost characteristics of the city. In fact, many of its landmarks are actually imitations of those in other cities – Tokyo Tower looks too much like the Eiffel Tower to truly represent Tokyo, Tokyo JR Station is a copy of the main station in Amsterdam and Tokyo Disneyland is a fantasyland designed to reproduce a fantasyland in, ahem, Southern California.

I find the concept of 'epitome districts' useful for understanding Tokyo. In the words of Grady Clay, these are parts of a city where "one can see the bigger place in compression or in miniature…special places in cities that carry huge layers of symbols and have the capacity to pack emotions, energy or history into a small place". Shinjuku, *shitamachi* and Sanya are such 'epitome districts' that reveal contrasting aspects of Tokyo society: consumerism, hard work, and hidden poverty.

In all of its history Tokyo has never stayed still for long, but has changed with every need and opportunity. In 1600, Ieyasu, the first Tokugawa shogun, took one look at Edo, the small fortress town that feudal lord Ōta Dōkan had built, and immediately began to rearrange it from top to bottom. He put in a new castle, realigned the flow of rivers, cut down Kanda Mountain and proceeded to fill in the marshes and parts of the bay. His successors continued the work, reclaimed still more land, expanded the city in new directions, and rebuilt its established districts time and again after every destructive fire or flood. In the late 19th century under the Meiji Emperor, there was a whole new face and new name – Tōkyō – that was given to the city as the nation's isolation ended and foreign fashions and building styles became the rage in the capital. The Taishō Emperor saw it all burn in 1923 after the Great Kantō Earthquake. Then just as soon as the city had been substantially rebuilt, there was war and the firebombing of 1945. Tokyo rose from those ashes, too, and in 1964 showed itself off to the world as a place of remarkable resilience and energy, as a city that wanted to be counted among the elite of global urban centres. It did not win many points for beauty as the world looked on during those Olympics, but it proved to everyone that it was workaholic and that it would build whatever was needed to advance its goals.

Now, a little more than 400 years after Ieyasu's arrival in the city, Tokyo has reached the top of the world economy and is changing again. This time the rebuilding is by choice rather than after some calamity, but is as complete and far-reaching as any undertaking before. It involves a huge range of projects, both private and public, that in various ways are intended to improve the quality of living in Tokyo and facilitate the needs of its important businesses, lavishing a completely new look upon the city. An important element of Tokyo's urban realignment is a grand strategy to remake the city into what planners call a 'multi-nodal metropolis' The idea is to relieve the Central Business District of some of its congestion and ease the heavy burden of hours of daily commuting by stimulating growth of commercial centres closer to where Tokyoites live. There are more than 20 emerging commercial nodes at key mass transit interchanges in the metropolis, the largest of which is at Shinjuku, a critical rail junction some six kilometres west of the CBD.

We can also understand the current rebuilding of Tokyo as one facet of what is being called 'internationalisation' or *kokusaika*. This is a common buzzword and refers simultaneously to different things:

1 the increasing influence that Japan has achieved among the nations;

2 the increased facility that many Japanese now have with foreign ways and languages; and

3 the growing presence of foreigners and foreign companies. It refers especially to still another aspect of internationalisation:

4 the rebuilding of Tokyo to make it more comfortable and more appealing to foreigners, particularly those with high-level business or diplomatic credentials. A key part is the construction of office buildings, hotels and other infrastructure to enhance Tokyo's standing as a leading international business centre. We see these goals expressed explicitly in development plans dictating that the city 'should be made a comfortable and friendly city for both foreign visitors and foreign residents', and that 'it is important to make Tokyo a safe, beautiful, comfortable and dignified city by increasing and improving parks, roads and other facilities, and shaping a tasteful cityscape'. All this, we are informed, is 'required in order to make Tokyo a truly international city that can lead the world in keeping up with the progress of internationalisation'.

In response to the complaints that foreigners most often make about Tokyo (high prices for everything from rent to a cup of coffee, chronic traffic jams and non-stop crowds, and typically small, somewhat primitive housing units), there are calculated efforts to put on a different face. Seeing an opportunity for profit, developers have put up great numbers of Western-style condominiums close to office districts and international embassies, also several new hotels and shopping designed to cater to the foreigner market as well as to Japanese with 'international' tastes.

The push to be international can be applied to virtually every aspect of the urban scene, including the most mundane. If I may be a bit irreverent, I can tell you about a fringe area of city planning that I had never considered before, that of toilet planning. Alerted by an intriguing notice in a newspaper, I once attended a daylong conference in Tokyo (and a field trip the next day) called the International Toilet Forum. Sponsored by the Japan Toilet Association of manufacturers, it had as its purpose an evaluation of toilet facilities in Tokyo from the standpoint of comfort for foreigners. There were sessions entitled 'Looking at Our International Cities – from Toilets' and 'Future Toilet Policies from an International Viewpoint', as well as a featured address by an architecture critic, Kawazoe Noboru, called 'Urban Planning – From the Toilet'. There was an amazing late afternoon session: 12 foreigners representing 12 different countries giving testimonials called 'My Experiences with Toilets' in which they compared public facilities in Japan with those back home. Everyone was perfectly serious, and I had the feeling that I was the only person among the 400 attendees who wanted to laugh. All the listeners were thoroughly professional and totally dedicated to the issue, behaving as if they were on some sort of sacred mission.

Despite the attention given to Tokyo's emerging international profile, it is important to point out that foreigners comprise only a small part of the total population. According to data for 2000, there were 278 358 foreign residents in *Tōkyō-to* as a whole, up from 121 663 in 1982 and 110 862 in 1978. While such numbers are large enough to make up the population of a small town, they represent only slightly more than 2 percent of the total for *Tōkyō-to*. What is more, nearly half of the foreigners in Tokyo were actually born in Japan, but they are counted as foreigners because their parents were not Japanese. Koreans and Chinese, who comprise 43.8 and 24.5 percent of the foreigner population, respectively, are the most numerous foreign populations. There are also several thousands from the Philippines, the United States, and Southeast and South Asian nations. The friendliness and hospitality extended to foreign residents and the many opportunities to form wonderful, lasting friendships is tempered by the knowledge that there are clear limits for foreigners, who forever remain outsiders. I remember my local dry-cleaner returning a suit to me with a tag in Japanese that identified me as *gaijin* #2, or 'foreigner #2'.

A popular guidebook begins with the observation that Japanese are people who 'love to spend and have the yen to do so'. It is easy to see the basis for this perception, because the city seems like an endless array of shopping centres and department stores, as well as restaurants of every imaginable cuisine and price range, countless bars, coffee shops, video arcades, *pachinko* parlours, and every other kind of business established that you can think of. Another successful guidebook, assembled by architect Richard S. Wurman, declared: "Tokyo is the world's largest department store. It aisles are subways and highways, filled with twice as many taxis and people as New York City. Its warehouse is the port and markets. Its business card is the multiple signature found in its neon skyline. Its jewellery department is the mechanical necklace created by the Yamanote line…".

The point is that Tokyo is an enormous market, and that this attribute is one of the key factors underlying its incessant building and rebuilding. In fact, it would be no exaggeration to state that shopping is one of the principal reasons for Tokyo's very existence: for example, historic Edo was transformed into a great urban centre only after Tokugawa Ieyasu had instituted policies to make it a capital of consumption. Specifically, Edo grew because it was an unprecedentedly large market for everything from stone for construction of the castle, to art objects for the mansions of *daimyō*, to fresh fish brought by boat to Nihombashi for sale to the public. Today, growth continues to be shaped by the city's role as Japan's capital of consumption, and much of the rebuilding that now defines it is done to stimulate consumption. A disproportionate amount of construction is made up of commercial centres: expansion of the CBD and of 'secondary' centres such as Shinjuku; construction of shopping plazas at virtually every train and subway station of any consequence.

The most striking scenes take place on Sundays, the principal shopping day, when literally millions of people take to the malls, cinemas, concert halls, theatres, museums, games arcades, restaurants and other places of consumer pleasure. Busy streets are closed to traffic and become jammed with pedestrians in great throngs among the stores. One can hardly move except to be carried by the wave of humanity and shopping bags. In the many bookstores crowds elbow for space at magazine racks to read about which new fashions to buy, or to learn which ski resorts or golf courses they should try, the best package deals for travel abroad, the schedule of Tokyo's movies and concerts, even the choice of foods at new restaurants. A ride on any subway reveals a consumer orientation. Everywhere the eye turns to avoid eye contact with other riders, there are posters that tout popular magazines (which themselves are filled with advertisements); upcoming TV programs (which will be interrupted again and again by still more commercial messages); schools that teach English; wedding chapels and reception halls; package tours to mountain spas and beach resorts; houses and condominiums in distant suburbs; tickets for concerts; sales. Even cemetery plots are promoted on trains, promising perpetual views of Mount Fuji.

Young people – of high school and college ages and young urban professionals – are especially visible as consumers. On the fashionable west side, almost all of them are impeccably dressed in expensive fashions and sport just the right accessories: designer handbags and backpacks, designer watches, designer sunglasses, mobile phones for couples to find each other in dense crowds. One of the most popular fashions is used clothing – American clothes once worn by strangers abroad. Young people feel an enormous pressure to be in step with such fashions and to have the requisite money. In the words of singing idol Matsutoya Yumi, famous for a brand of 'new music' (*nyu-muzziku*) that reflects the culture of suburban youth, "When I run out of money that is when I die. There is no other way, really. If you take away the economic power from what I want to do, there's nothing left at all." For many, the money comes from affluent parents, themselves spend-happy consumers. Others work seemingly endless hours at *arubaito* ("Arbeit", part-time jobs) to earn spending money. It seems that they toil for hours on one side of a counter selling hamburgers, clothing or accessories, just for the chance to cross to the other side and buy them. The growing problem of shoplifting is mostly unreported because shopkeepers do not want to lose face with customers, but evidence that theft is rising is seen in the proliferation of surveillance cameras, anti-theft sensors, and uniformed security guards.

A particularly distressing development is an enormous upsurge in prostitution by teenage girls for the specific purpose of getting money to buy consumer luxuries. Referred to as *enjo kōsai*, 'compensated dates', the typical pattern is for high-school girls to make appointments with middle-aged 'salarymen' through telephone clubs, charging them hundreds of thousands of yen for a single liaison in a 'love-hotel'. As one such 16-year-old girl explained casually in a newspaper interview about her craving for Louis Vuitton bags and Chanel perfume, "Girls in my school tend to be split up into the girls who have such things and girls who don't. If you have the brand-name things, you're important". Another young girl who has entered this economy explained her situation very matter-of-factly, "I prostitute to get tickets for concerts by famous musicians. I am not wrong. It's the price of the tickets that is wrong".

The Imperial Palace will always remain the spiritual centre of Tokyo; adjacent districts such as Marunouchi and Nihombashi will always be thought of as the traditional centres of economic power. However, Shinjuku has emerged as a formidable commercial nucleus, laying legitimate claims to being the new principal centre of *Tōkyō-to* (Tokyo Metropolis). Already, Shinjuku Station is far and away the busiest station in the city (and for that matter in the world), handling more than 3 million passengers each day (in comparison to the 0.7 million who pass through Tokyo JR Station) Other distinctions include having most of the tallest buildings, being the number-one retailing centre, housing some of the best hotels and the biggest and best-known nighttime entertainment districts. Furthermore, since 1991 Shinjuku has been the site of the government centre of Tokyo Metropolis. The new city hall complex is an elaborate and imposing edifice, exuding authority and dominating its surroundings much like Edo Castle did when Tokyo was young.

The skyline of Shinjuku is represented in Japanese film and TV as the setting for big-city detective adventures, and the backdrop for commercial advertising for various 'urban-sophisticated' products: cigarettes, whisky and luxury cars. This has resulted in Shinjuku's becoming the most widely recognised urban scene. Emulation of New York is quite direct. I have a Christmas card illustrating the Shinjuku skyline on a quiet snowy night (both quiet and snow are rare), Santa plus reindeer in the sky above, and the unmistakable reflection of the Statue of Liberty on the glass skin of a high-rise. Statues of Liberty are also seen atop some 'love-hotels'. I also have a key chain that says 'Tokyo Megalopolis' and shows a montage of Tokyo's landmarks and NY's Chrysler Building. There is also a new shopping centre called "Times Square" and an artificial waterfall in its own "Central Park" called "Niagara Falls".

Shinjuku displays the dazzling side of Tokyo capitalism: it is a world of flashing neon; of giant billboards and multi-storey advertising banners; of commercial jingles blaring non-stop; of hard-sell claims about 'low, low prices' from touts with megaphones; and of every type and size and fashion of store, restaurant, bar or other commercial establishment imaginable. It is larger than Ginza and other traditional commercial nodes, larger than all the other giant shopping centres scattered in all directions. Comparative statistics are hard to come by, but the east side of Shinjuku Station alone does more retail trade than number-two ranking Ginza (€ 0.5 billion versus € 0.42 billion already in the mid-80s), Shinjuku's west side is third in the metropolis, and the two 'halves' of Shinjuku combined have long pulled away from the competition and are becoming ever more dominant. Its most significant retail businesses include several of Tokyo's largest camera and electronics emporiums, and a seemingly endless array of boutiques, accessory shops, and fashion outlets, much of it under ground level. The famous Mitsukoshi and Isetan department stores are both present with their own art galleries and museums, centres of sophisticated culture. Their routines include cultural programming and shopping during the day for prosperous housewives from neighbourhoods served by Shinjuku's train lines. On Sundays, Shinjuku-dōri is closed to vehicular traffic. From noon until dinner time the street is jammed with families spending their one free day of the week together in the shops, as well as young couples and hordes of fashion-minded teenagers and pre-teens.

The area close to Shinjuku Station is also the site of many types of eating and drinking establishments, often with meaningless Western names. They serve shoppers and also reflect a natural symbiosis with the other business functions of Shinjuku. Many of the restaurants serve breakfasts to the first arrivals in Shinjuku, the *asagata ningen* or 'early-morning crowd', who prefer to get a jump-start at work before the trains overfill or who will soon be opening the stores. It is common to see individuals dozing behind a newspaper in a breakfast place. Naturally, lunch is big business, as is delivering meals to workers too busy to leave their offices. One sees small motorbikes specially equipped with carrying devices for food, most notably for bowls of noodles. A special category of cafe, *kissaten*, serves coffee and snacks during the day to customers who use them as venues for business meetings, private rendezvous, or for a quiet rest. The popularity of *kissaten* is due to the lack of privacy in overcrowded offices, and accessibility to train stations that bring the different parties in for a meeting together.

Still another category is busiest at the end of the day when people go out for dinner and drinks. Their design is especially set up for groups. This is because it is a common practice in Japan for co-workers to go out together *en masse* after office, and because reunions from schools and clubs often come together at convenient transit centres. The reason that so many people can fit into Shinjuku is that much of the restaurant business is arranged vertically, often in tall, slender buildings that contain nothing other than places for food and drink.

There is one sub-district of Shinjuku that is more distinctive than all the others. Kabukicho, located a few minutes' walk north-east of the station, is itself an 'epitome district' that speaks volumes about how Tokyo works and about the intricacies of certain aspects of Japanese society. Here is a place that is much more than just the largest, bawdiest entertainment district: it is a gigantic fantasyland for adults, a total escape for tens of thousands from all the ills and oppressions that surround them. It is most famous for its most imaginative sex businesses: hostess clubs, strip shows, peepshow parlours, 'no-panties coffee shops', pornography emporiums, and special massage parlours that Japanese now call 'soaplands' (the original name *toruko-buro* – Turkish baths – was dropped after complaints from the Turkish embassy). A lot of what goes on is just downright kinky. Prostitution has been illegal since 1957, but it thrives in this setting nonetheless. There are also a great many 'legitimate' diversions: restaurants and bars with every kind of cuisine and decor imaginable, movie houses, bowling alleys, video arcades, *pachinko* parlours and *karaoke* clubs. They attract a varied clientele that includes women and students in addition to carousing "salarymen" Nevertheless, for many Tokyoites, the uncounted legions who wouldn't set foot there because of its reputation, the place is not an escape from problems at all – it is one of the problems. For them, as well as for foreigner observers, Kabukicho represents some of the worst of Japan: rampant exploitation of women, both Japanese and foreign, as well as widespread excessive drunkenness, gambling, and gangsterism.

The busiest time in Kabukicho begins at dusk when the streets come aglow with neon. Huge crowds of customers, just released from work or from school, cross traffic-choked Yasukuni-dōri and descend on its thousand places of pleasure. They are beckoned by flashing signs of every shape and colour, by tall columns of neon that run the height of buildings with the names of pubs, by touts carrying signs and calling out invitations, by scantily clad bar girls in the doorways smiling at likely prospects, and by fantasyland architecture that ranges from medieval European castles to a giant mechanical crab affixed to a seafood restaurant that claws at the attentions of passers-by. A special subsection, Golden-gai, packed together in a quarter of a city block, is a maze of some 240 tiny establishments, some no bigger than three or four bar stools. The buildings are seedy and falling apart. Perhaps because they appear to be in imminent danger of being urban-renewed away, and because they look dangerous, like the haunts of TV gangsters, that it has become a mark of prestige in the night world of Tokyo to be welcome there and to have a seat among regulars.

Still another area, the secluded far side of Kabukicho, specialises in 'love hotels' that rent rooms by the hour to couples on dates and furtive office romances, and to married couples who lack privacy. They are busy during the day, too, especially during the Sunday afternoon leisure time that is so much a part of the Japanese routine. The architectural design of love hotels and their guestrooms emphasises fantasy. Themes from foreign lands and past eras such as fairyland castles and 50s movies are especially common.

Not all of Tokyo is so consumer oriented. People work incredibly hard, often for low wages at more than one job, simply to meet basic living expenses. For thousands of Tokyoites, it is a challenge to pay the rent on time and have enough left over for food and transportation, and unthinkable to have designer wares or expensive vacations. Many students work at odd jobs principally to pay tuition and buy books, and keep any travel plans as dreams for the future. In fact, some sections of the city stand in direct contrast to the glitzy districts of Tokyo's west side, and can be seen principally as places of difficult work and unadorned living. A short distance east or north of the city's centre, approaching the Sumida River, we come to *shitamachi* (the 'low city'), Tokyo's old plebeian section. It is much more of a private and unassuming district than the flashy Shinjuku side, but is nonetheless very much alive and a fully integral part of Tokyo. Because change is slow here and has taken different directions to that in other parts, *shitamachi* is nostalgically referred to as 'the real Tokyo'. It is where the most traditional aspects are still visible. There are also distinct contrasts in economic base, social characteristics, and physical conditions of the living environment.

The most striking impression is that here is truly a part of the city given over to work. Other places are busy too, in fact extremely so as we have seen in Shinjuku, but in this case the work is of a type that all those other centres depend on before they themselves can begin; the foundation for the rest of the economy. It is home to thousands of unheralded companies at the broad base of the pyramid, supporting the enterprises of big corporations above them and the routines of the more conspicuous districts. Among a hundred other distinctions, this is where the taxi drivers that serve the centre of the city come from; the central place where fresh seafood is sold and distributed; where the city's newspapers, magazines, business cards (*meishi*), and the indispensable cheap comic books for commuters (*manga*) are printed; the factory zone where boxes and wrapping papers are made for manufacturers and retailers; and where the advertising tissue packets are put together that pretty girls press into your hands at busy train stations. There are warehouses; wholesale companies; transportation facilities: truck and bus terminals, rail sidings, and piers; dispatching centres for delivery services; and a great many factories and shops of all sizes, but mostly small.

An unexpected side of Tokyo is the intimate scale and almost village-like atmosphere of many districts. There is strong feeling of community in similar neighbourhoods all over the city. The street is a friendly place where hundreds of conversations take place, and a play space for children. Merchants' associations (*chōkai*) make sure of seasonal decorations and loudspeakers mounted on utility poles churning out popular tunes. One spring I watched with pleasure as *chōkai* members took down plastic snowflakes and replaced them with plastic cherry blossoms.

Tsukiji district in *shitamachi* was the site of a foreigner's compound in the 19th century. Now, however, it is *Tōkyō no daidokoro*, 'Tokyo's pantry'. This is where some 14 000 restaurateurs, sushi chefs, and retail fishmongers come each day to the vast and impressive fish market to purchase their daily supply. They shop at one or other of 1677 stalls, most of them tiny, family-run operations, competing fiercely for business within the confines of a centralised market set up in 1935. All night long, trucks with fresh seafood arrive from fishing ports all over Japan and from Narita Airport, the biggest fishing port of all. Auctions start at 5:30 a.m. and end soon after. The careful inspection of rows after rows of huge tuna, arranged like gleaming torpedoes in the dawn light, by buyers who peer with flashlights inside deep incisions is an unforgettable sight. Purchases are taken by barrow to be cut and resold at one of the stalls, or to make deliveries to supermarkets and other retail outlets. Many purchasers pedal away on bicycles, headed for the sushi shops of Ginza and Shimbashi, with full polystyrene crates stacked one atop another and strapped precariously on the back. The rest of the morning is given to retailing.

There is one neighbourhood within this 'other side of Tokyo' that is so different from the rest that it needs to be considered separately. It is called Sanya, Tokyo's closest equivalent to a slum. Located in Taito and Arakawa Wards, it is a place few people know and that no one goes to except those who live there. It is the secret 'underside of Tokyo', a place inhabited largely by the cast-offs of society and ignored by almost everyone else. Even most maps of the city fail to identify it, and either use formal *chome* place names only or, more often, are designed to superimpose boxed map titles or legends over where Sanya would have been. I know of an instance in which a Japanese TV-crew that had previously covered combat in SE Asia refused to go in there because of fear. Sanya has been a hidden section of Tokyo since early in the Edo era, when its ground became poisoned forever as the shogun's site for executions of lawbreakers and opponents. There was once a bridge across a small stream at Sanya's entrance where relatives of the condemned said their farewells; the bridge and waterway are gone now, but the street intersection at the site bears the name Namidabashi, "Bridge of Tears."

That there is also a Sanya in every other big city in the world is beside the point. I include it not just to represent Tokyo more fully but also to stress that even here, at the very bottom of the scale, the city is shaped by powerful traditions and unchanging beliefs. Not all of Tokyo's homeless live in Sanya, and not all of them are day labourers or alcoholics. Homelessness is now a much larger problem, affecting thousands of men and women, many other neighbourhoods, and having many causes. What is more, it seems to be getting worse – at least since the start of the 1990s when the so-called 'bubble economy' burst. Like Sanya itself, homelessness is another of those uncomfortable topics that official statistics fail to acknowledge and few Japanese want to discuss – a 'hidden' problem that is plainly evident because many of the homeless are, almost literally, 'underfoot' in the city's busiest districts such as Shinjuku.

It is not known exactly how many homeless people there are. The official estimate is 3000, but that total seems low given the number of homeless people one routinely sees. A more realistic estimate, offered by T.D. Guzewicz and the Salvation Army, is 10 000, but even that might be too low, given the rapid growth of the problem and the fact that many of the homeless hide in out-of-the-way places. The number of homeless people changes from year to year in response to turns in the economy, or with the seasons, being related to cycles in agricultural labour.

The situation in Shinjuku deserves special mention. After Ueno, it has the largest concentration of homeless, in the range of several thousand individuals. It is also the city's most visible concentration of homeless, clustered in Shinjuku Station and the labyrinthine underground corridors that lead to it, in plain view of the millions of commuters who pass by each day. The underground provides protection from bad weather, access to lavatories, and resources ranging from leftover food discarded by restaurants to a plentiful supply of current magazines left behind in trains. About 200 of the homeless reside on Shinjuku Station's west side, amid heavy pedestrian traffic, in a tidy settlement made of cardboard boxes. Some of the dwellings have more than one 'room', are equipped with futons, a few basic kitchen items, and ropes for drying laundry. Calendars hang from cardboard walls, giving an added sense of permanence and domesticity. Some of its denizens earn small incomes reselling salvaged magazines or partly used telephone cards. Others are paid by ticket scalpers to stand in queues to purchase concert tickets. No one begs, even though there are plenty of passersby who could be approached. In fact, there is little contact of any kind, including eye contact, between Shinjuku's shantytown dwellers and the throngs of shoppers, commuters and evening revellers who pass by each day.

In January 1995 Shinjuku was the scene of a dramatic confrontation between homeless people and police. Approximately 200 homeless people living in cardboard boxes aligned along an underground passageway were forcibly removed by as many as 820 police, security guards and government officials. The 6 a.m. raid, timed to be concluded before the crush hour, followed earlier warnings because of plans to construct a moving walkway connecting Shinjuku station with the new City Hall. Many of the evictees responded by throwing bottles, eggs and flour, setting off fire extinguishers, chaining themselves to posts and locking arms in resistance. The incident was front-page news across the nation and in many newspapers abroad. Not only was there the irony that people were being moved for a people mover, but the incident made public some topics about which Japan had been reticent: that homelessness is a growing problem in this rich country, that it is not simply the result of alcohol addiction or mental illness, but increasingly is tied to unemployment and other economic problems; and that the city has little idea what to do about it.

Tokyo, thus, is composed of many different places, each with its own story and its own distinctive character. All these faces of the metropolis illustrate its unsurpassed dynamism, up-front modernity coupled in a curious way with age-old attitudes. Certainly more than any other urban centre I know, this city is process, not artefact.

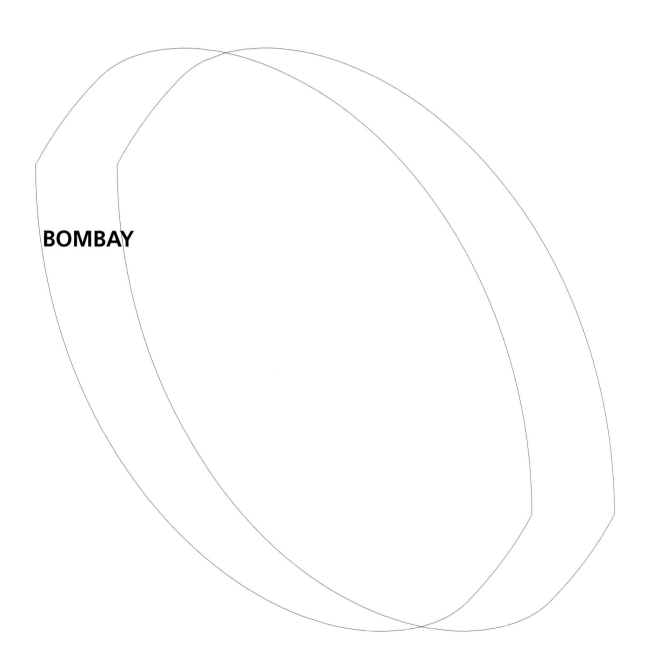

BOMBAY

The storms of globalisation have been blowing through this port since its founding, mercilessly determining the politics and livelihood even of its opponents. Bombay survives its vast problems and succeeds in being global because it layers different times and world-views and manages to transcend them all.

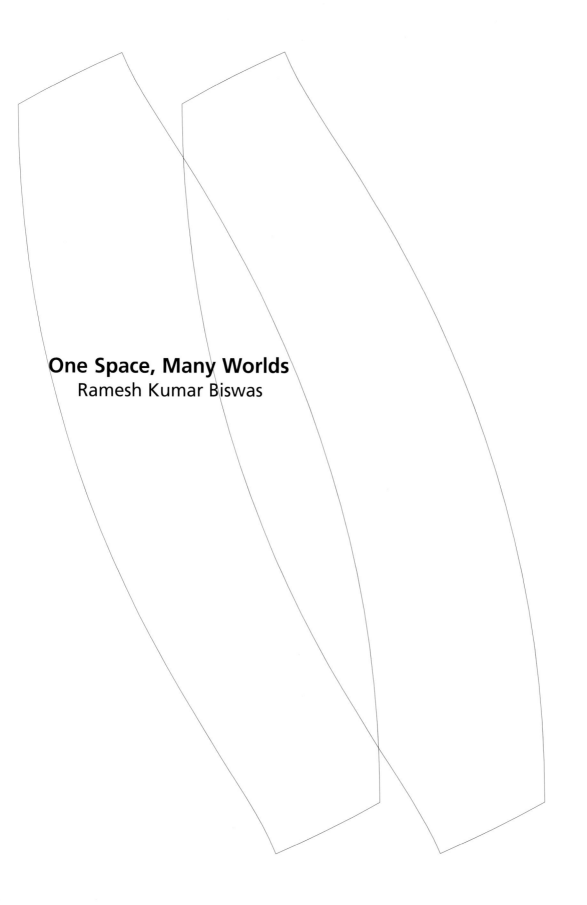

One Space, Many Worlds
Ramesh Kumar Biswas

When someone at a cocktail party wants to illustrate the worst possible conglomeration to be in, the punishment-posting to dread, the most commonly named are Ciudad de Mexico, Calcutta, Cairo and Bombay. Yet Bombay is a city much loved by its inhabitants and worshipped by the thousands of hopeful who stream there every day from all over the country, very few of whom will ever leave. Poverty, misery, ugliness, chaos, pollution and brown polyester safari-suits: the usual shuddered experiences of the horrors of Bombay tend to obscure the view of a city that unites the vast and wonderful variety of India and adds quite a few glittering facets of its own. It is a difficult place full of delights, marvels and mysteries. How is one to read Bombay? How do Indians see their future and the future of their cities? What can one say about a city whose 18 million inhabitants insist on speaking 150 languages and eating 240 kinds of leavened bread?

BOMBAY

It is a characteristic of Occidental society that it wants to, no, *has* to know other worlds. The West (Paul Valery once thoughtfully considered it *"l'cap d'Asie"*) never was self-sufficient. The Revelation, the Stone of Wisdom, and the Source of Eternal Life, the Cradle of Humanity, Paradise, Eldorado or the Golden Age was always elsewhere, eastwards. It is striking that if there is one place which has attracted seekers since the days of the ancients, it is the *mirabilia indiae*, a land full of monsters and miracles, yet accessible, personally familiar, part of the old Euro-Asian world. Columbus and Vasco de Gama were sent out not to discover new worlds but to re-establish lost Eurasian connections through new sea routes.

There are cities in India are which are the graveyards of dynasties, where the dust of centuries lies heavy on the eyelids. Bombay is not one of these. Indian tradition sets out a course that every human must traverse. According to the ancient texts this path through life is marked by four stations: *dharma* (duty, learning), *artha* (material life), *kama* (sensual pleasures) and *moksha* (salvation). One could interpret certain cities to represent one or the other of these stages, as crystallised Hindu philosophy: Varanasi (Benares), for example, is clearly a spiritual city and thus associated with *moksha*.

Bombay is not primarily a city of sensuality or lust, though it has huge red-light districts, where lanky American sociologists toting tape recorders almost outnumber the prostitutes. Bombay is almost by definition the city of *artha*, of money and power. It is the *de facto* capital of the Republic. With only one and a half percent of the country's population, it supplies 40% of its tax revenue. While Delhi is "the capital of the missed appointment, the wrong number and the punctured tyre", as Jan Morris puts it, Bombay strives to be efficient and dynamic.

Although the once imposing textile industry has all but collapsed under the burden of low productivity, strikes and poor management; jobs in information technologies are snowballing. Economic growth rates are only exceeded by certain SE Asian capitals. Contrary to widespread belief, the overwhelming majority of IT firms are located in Bombay, not in Bangalore. The diamond exchange rivals that of Antwerp. The stock market is the fourth largest in Asia (after rising from a market capitalisation of only €7.5 billion in 1980 to €84 billion today). Bombay may not yet be a key factor in the globalised world, but it has definitely been global for a long time. Delhi is officially the seat of federal political power, but in Bombay economic power rules – it houses most of the nation's industry, financial services, insurance companies and half of all foreign or joint ventures, the Reserve Bank with its mint, several Arab banks, the country's biggest container harbour handling half the total port traffic, the most web users, the press establishment and a fecund movie business known as Bollywood, all of which are more influential and effective in forming the city than regional or central political bodies. The private sector dominates and steers urban life to a greater degree than the overburdened authorities. When a recent judicial investigation revealed connections between a leading stockbroker, organised crime and a former member of the government, I was taken aback – it was the first time I had heard of the government being connected to *anything* organised.

Although the collection of corporate towers on reclaimed land on Nariman point do represent big money, a more traditional manifestation of *artha* is the bazaar, which encompasses the entire spectrum of trade. The bazaar in the old town is not restricted to a main square, rather it draws you into the dozens of crooked lanes branching off in all possible directions. Sales, trade and repairs take place in the innumerable workshops and shops. Head-massages with ear-cleanings, safari-suits made to order against all tenets of good taste, studio photographs in "Three Different Poses with Three Different Modern Dresses", Polish vodka made solely for export to Poland, colourful statues of helpful goddesses, lizard-oil cures for erectile reluctance, Rajasthan-School miniatures in Bombay-Tourist-School, furniture dealers with Fake-Antique-Departments, holy men producing unnecessary quantities of ash from their foreheads, unbearably sweet sweets, cows placidly chewing plastic carrier bags, babies wailing in ninety dialects, eunuchs singing tunelessly, old men muttering *ram ram ram ram*.

The bazaars are a spectacle of Hell even for many local residents, and most middle-class urban dwellers in India would admit that they have never been to their respective old town centres. They strive towards a clean and rational environment and take pains to avoid the impenetrable maze of the old India. As it happens, it is this very appearance of chaos that has protected traditional Indian cultures from destruction by conquerors with other views, such as the British – or even the Western-oriented Indian upper classes. For those in power understood not what they saw, and named it chaos, the jungle. They built their headquarters, their administrative centres and their barracks somewhere else on green fields, and thus spared the bazaar from destruction. But what looked like chaos was, in fact, complexity, a multi-layered order, systems superimposed on each other or existing next to each other. These ordering systems were totally comprehensible to those participating in them and frightening to those outside. Only the actors ever changed. The functions and the activities were always fixed – every square centimetre of the bazaar was defined with regard to who could use it, what one could do there, when one could do it and to what purpose – and the community made sure that the rules were kept. Far from being chaotic, this is actually a highly organised society with dos and don'ts that would intimidate a suburbanite in Cherry Hill, New Jersey.

A fascinating example of this complex order is the globally unique system for the distribution of office lunches that has existed here for decades. Indians are notorious for their intricate food taboos that dictate what to eat, with whom, and when not to eat. There are different varieties of vegetarians: those who eat eggs but don't touch garlic, others who do not partake of onions but accept milk, yet others to whom you can say nothing but "have some nuts". Because it was difficult to cater to these needs, there were very few restaurants, and even those who could afford them could not be sure of what they were being served, or who had prepared it. Thus, to be on the safe side, the God-fearing working man ate only his mother's or his wife's cooking. But he left for work too early for her to have something freshly cooked for him – besides the food would go cold till lunchtime. So the housewife cooked the midday meal after her husband had left for work, a courier collected it in a small aluminium tiffin carrier and took it to the suburban station where it, and each of the millions of other such tin boxes, was coded with a series of strange hieroglyphs (most of the food couriers being illiterate). It was then taken by commuter trains, empty at noon, into the centre of town, stacked up spectacularly with a myriad tiffin boxes from all the other suburbs on the platforms under the steel vaulted roof of Victoria Station; where it was then picked up by another courier who got it to the right person's desk in the right office on the dot. Complex logistics and punctuality were demanded several million times over, day after day, no mistakes could take place between the suburbs and the centre, between the kitchen and the office table. No beef to be handed by mistake to a Hindu, no pork to a Muslim, no garlic to a Jain. And you call this a chaotic city?

Today even this system is disappearing – there are very few housewives, as most women work, too. Cheap eating places have sprung up everywhere, food taboos are on their way out and the business lunch on its way in. No doubt the food couriers will come up with some other unique, unheard of and strangely useful service only they can provide, in the historically typical, entrepreneurial, Bombay way.

This is a city that you should not dismiss even if something does not work out or you are kept on a futile wait. The ever accelerating urban dimensions and the changing qualities of time govern our lives and reveal much about the cities in which we live. Look beyond the surface and you will discover a city here that runs on different rhythms and, though young, incorporates several era in it: colonial, traditional and modern. A city where time is a series of phantoms, realities and myths. Where the ticking of the wristwatch is overlaid with the beat of archaic drums, different *tablas*. Any cheap Bombay calendar bought on the street would illustrate, with its intricate overlapping of Vedic, Gregorian, Buddhist and Islamic cycles, the complexity of simultaneous existences that a Bombay resident lives through every day. It runs partly on a popular ritual time, a stellar time determined by horoscopes, which recommend the right moment for a wedding, a business deal or a move to a new apartment. It also runs on a cosmic time signalled by lunar cycles which declare religious festivals, and days of fasting and abstinence, all of which have precedence over banal human activities such as work. 'Lifetime' is based on the four stations in life mentioned earlier. 'Linguistic time' has its own fluid qualities in Sanskrit-based languages where the word for tomorrow is the same as that for yesterday, and the words for day-after-tomorrow and day-before-yesterday are identical. There is an epic time, which proclaims our age (*kaliyuga*) to be one of decline and destruction, and which demands sacrifices to appease the gods. There is Indian Standard Time, based on a longitude running through Delhi and valid for the entire sub-continent. Indian Standard Time is itself a joke phrase that Indians use to refer to their own notorious impunctuality. Furthermore, there is solar time, which determines the working day and the pleasures of the night, there is the rotation of the earth that sets shipping dates for this busily exporting centre. And then there is internet time related to many time zones, crucial for Bombay's survival as an on-line city. Watching a typical scene of people going about their daily duties in this city, a scene that looks as if it were an unspecified disaster movie being projected at the wrong speed, one must keep all this in mind to understand the way Bombay moves.

The archipelago of seven islands on which the city stands today was handed over to the British by the Portugese in 1661, in the casual way that colonial powers had in those days when dealing with other peoples' countries. The main trading post of the British East India Company was transferred there 26 years later. In the 18th century the islands were joined by landfill and two zones were created: the Fort area for the rulers, at the tip of the peninsula, and an area for locals variously called "New Town", "Bazaar Zone" or even "Native Town". Mercantile activity (silks, diamonds, tea and opium) and, later, industrial development (textiles) followed once the British had managed to attract traditional business communities of different castes and religions from the hinterland. Cotton exports boomed in the 1860s during the American Civil War (which was loudly booming in its own way). "The city which by God's assistance is intended to be built", as the colonial masters proclaimed it, was steadily asserting its place not just as India's first city, but also, after 1872, as the second city in the Empire after London. People went there from Britain and its colonies as well as from the rest of the subcontinent in the hope of finding wealth and success, and of never again having to read provincial newspaper headlines like "Municipal Councillor Opens Much-Needed Roundabout In Front Of Canning Factory".

Great institutions such as the elite Bombay University were established. Then came the traumatic Partition of the subcontinent in 1947, which led to an exodus of the some of the Muslim community and a major influx of Hindus and Christians from Karachi. As the geographer Heinz Nissel has documented, after a period of overcrowding culminating in the 1960s (landlords subdivided their downtown properties into a maximum of tiny cells to make a profit in spite of rent control regulations), with its attendant miseries and epidemics, the increasingly commercial use of the land on the Peninsula and upward-spiralling rents (higher in absolute terms than in Manhattan) led to a radical decrease in its residential population. People moved: north up the coast; north-west towards the airport, once outside town but now central; and eastwards to the twin city of New Bombay on the mainland across the bay. As most people still work in the

Central or the Fort areas, and new sub-centres are only just developing, this dispersion has led to a massive loss of time for commuters, who often spend up to five hours a day travelling to and from suburbs up to 100 km away. Mobility and flexibility are evidently not just slogans for the Bombayite. Bombay has had a long history of conscious and idealistic urban planning which has continuously tried to ameliorate conditions, but the massive influx of job-seekers from villages (which still house three-fourths of the country's population and hence remain an endless source of future migrants) is testing the limits of traditional planning recipes. The urban designer Rahul Mehrotra tells of visiting planners from abroad who talk about revitalising central areas, to which he answers in despair, "No revitalising, please! On the contrary, we need to calm down these places!"

The hot and sticky city awaits the monsoon, that singular deluge that first brings people out dancing in the streets and then has them scurrying for shelter. The monsoon forces even the business-suited to take off their shoes and roll up their trousers to wade knee deep in the flood-water on the streets. (The Indus Valley cities to the north had functioning canals and drainage systems 5500 years ago. Unfortunately they did not pass on their expertise to present-day Bombay urban services).

The heavy rains are not façade-friendly. On the street one passes new buildings that almost immediately look shabby and run down, interspersed with sudden ruins with steel reinforcements sticking out like punk hairdos. It is difficult to detect if such structures are still under construction or momentarily being demolished. Bollywood may have 'enhanced' the brightness of Technicolour, Bombay's builders have done the reverse for architecture. There are entire blackened and crumbling blocks of houses which are puzzling: a bomb blast? gang warfare? a religious riot? a gas explosion? or merely bad planning?

The physical structure of the city is not pleasing; in fact, the material reality of Bombay is so unattractive that we have to look elsewhere for the city's fascination. "Every day that Bombay becomes worse as a physical environment", says Charles Correa, renowned architect and co-planner of New Bombay, "it becomes better as a city". Architectural triumphs are indeed rare, and one would have to reduce one's own aesthetic standards considerably in order to consider the monstrous and gloomy Victorian piles built by the British as worthy monuments. The surviving Art Deco buildings are barely recognisable under the grime. Indian society tends to lose its creativity by superficially copying western aesthetics, on the other hand, the world finds it difficult to understand the symbolic content of Indian aesthetics. Here it is not the form itself, but what it represents that matters. In this vacuum curiosities come into being. The 3000 year old city of Varanasi can hardly bear the weight of its architectural jewellery, but Bombay is an Indian version of the Eurovision Song Contest: it has no masterpieces – it is more a laboratory for the fusion of multiple identities.

In Julian Barne's novel 'England, England', a smart businessman sets up a concentrated collection of the sights of England – Buckingham Palace, Trafalgar Square, Kew Gardens, Stonehenge – in a little park on the Isle of Wight, to offer tourists a quintessence of England. But anyone who thinks that Bombay is a similarly conceived authentic synopsis of India to be conveniently visited on a small area, merely because Indians from all over the country live here, is mistaken. Shortly after their arrival in Bombay they begin to discard their traditional dress, loyalties, caste and mother tongue. Bombay throws its 'huddled masses' into its cauldron and stirs them energetically. Even the apparently absurd Bollywood film has done much to implant a revolutionary, progressive idea into the minds of young people: that they can actually choose their partners themselves, and that it is not necessarily left to divine law, the wisdom of one's parents or the effectiveness of matrimonial ads. Bombay has done more to reduce discrimination based on caste, religion or sex than all the state's anti-discrimination policies put together. A Brahmin can no longer avoid living or working next to "untouchables" or being squeezed between them in a crowded bus. The urban transformation is even more radical than a move to New York, where new migrants traditionally first look for shelter and work in their ethnic group area. In Bombay one is on one's own. The niches that each one finds – and tries to leave again as soon as possible – have no easy access. The local configurations of an average small town in India (which could well be a settlement of millions) are traditionally based on the readable coordinates of religion, caste, occupation

and power. These indicators are not clearly visible in Bombay. Yes, of course, the towers on reclaimed land at Nariman Point house only national and multinational business concerns, and you would be hard put to find poverty-stricken residents of Malabar Hills, but the converse assumption, that there are no rich people to be found in Dahravi, which has the doubtful honour of being the biggest slum in Asia, would not be correct. Of course, there are people in the film industry who showcase their wealth in the most vulgar possible fashion, but Bombay also has figures like the beggar who died sometime ago, who spent his days on the steps of an office block on Marine Drive, the most expensive location in town, thankfully collecting the coins that were thrown his way. After his death, his will revealed the astonishing fact that he was the owner of the building in front of which he had been begging. It is also common for a successful businessman to continue to stay in the slum-like tenement in which he was born. One layer covers the other in a manner impossible to decipher.

Bombay is a place where you can search for many things: for the Indian identity (if it exists at all and if it is of any use); for the global role of a megacity; and for the possibility of a socially and environmentally acceptable balance in the megalopolis that will ensure the continued existence of mankind. Novelist Arundhati Roy's answer is, "Let us say that we are old people that are learning to live in a nation of recent date." This applies above all to Bombay, which is going through a violent process of "*Mumbaiisation*", political demand for power for the people from the surrounding state of Maharashtra. Bombay is becoming more provincial and chauvinistic at the same time that it is becoming more international. These are parallel processes full of contradictions. It has been going through the joys and pains of globalisation on a small scale for several decades already and is now going through its backlash. The very city that has always accepted the persecuted and the daring:

Parsis and Bahais from Persia, Anglo-Asians from the colonies, European Jews, Armenians, traders from Arabia; a city many of whose residents have relatives in other countries and whose upper classes frequently exercise their privilege of travelling abroad; a city that is truly on-line to the world, where corporations like Swissair have moved their ticketing operations and Siemens develops its software; has witnessed the revolt of nationalists and chauvinists. Now that they wield power, they have begun to realise themselves that they cannot cut Bombay off from the rest of the world.

The debate about renaming the city is an illustration of this conflict. The word Bombay comes from the Portuguese "*bombaim*" (good harbour), but local chauvinist parties arbitrarily chose a mascot, *Mumbadevi*, patron goddess of fishermen, and rechristened (or re-Hinduised in this case) the city "*Mumbai*" (as a side effect, Bollywood became "Mollywood"). The national government subsequently decreed that the word Bombay would continue to be the sole valid name for national administration purposes and for international use. Although many media have jumped on to the political "*Mumbai*" bandwagon, a significant part of the population rejects the new name – since the city is not just reverting to a traditional name that was difficult for the erstwhile colonial masters to pronounce – because they see it as an unacceptable frontal attack on the cosmopolitan nature of the city.

But was the city ever really as cosmopolitan as it has been touted to be? The truth is that two societies coexist in the same space – one is a somewhat Westernised middle-class of educated urbanites; and the other is a more numerous group that represents rural and regional Indian society. Both these groups display their typical strengths and weaknesses. While the first has discarded most of its traditions and customs in favour of greater global opportunities and wealth, the second, more integrated group has tended to become resentful, stifling and slavishly conservative. The chasm between them has deepened. While it is obvious that Bombay has a levelling effect, these two worlds did not even seem to share the same space until events forced them to become aware of one another. The upper ten percent earns multiples of the average €60 that the lowest three-quarters earn annually. I once visited an Bombay industrialist in his mansion full of Venetian chandeliers, Chinese and English antiques, Impressionists and Picassos, with a driveway parked with Duisenbergs, Mercedes and Rolls' from the 20s and 30s ("Envy", he proclaimed, "is a low emotion"), while a couple of hundred metres from his guarded gate I saw men wading waist-deep in a sewer, salvaging junk that even the slum-dwellers next to it had deemed fit to throw away.

The real political revolution in Bombay during the last few years is that power is once again coming from the bazaar, the slums and the pavements, where over 60% of the city's residents live – a cry of protest from the (presumably or actually) colonised, disenfranchised 'original' resident. For many Bombayites and outsiders, this came as a total shock – they never expected anything like the bloody riots and slaughter of minorities to happen in what they considered the most open-minded and unfettered city on the subcontinent. But Bombay's political change of profile had gone far beyond a few terrible riots. Deep changes have been taking place under the surface. The political establishment had neglected the huge constituency of the have-nots (or the have-not-enoughs). The deprived 7.4 million slum-dwellers and the 950 000 pavement dwellers, with limited rights, money or dignity, were being steadily mobilised by Hindu-fundamentalist and linguistically chauvinist groups who did much more than just hold meetings (though street theatre has long been a backbone of Marathi literature, initially used by left-wing idealists to enlighten and modernise the masses, later by right-wing parties to transmit their ethnocentric agenda). They also set up a functioning network of privately-funded and volunteer-staffed social services, so that when poor people in slums fall ill at night, there are ambulances to take them to hospital, something that had never been done for them before. They organised jobs, courses and the provision of infrastructure: electricity, roads and water, things that well-meaning but totally overburden local authorities and international aid agencies had been unable to provide equitably. And the network of loyalties they built up provided a political platform which enabled them to win mayoral and state elections in the 1990s.

This city is blessed with more than a thousand large slums, whose huge population occupies only 3% of the urban area and therefore reaches a sardine-tin density of 370 000 per sq km. These migrants are too poor to commute to work and lack the qualifications to find 'proper' jobs in the city, hence the extremely high rate of self-employment or group-work within their own slums (ref. Nissel, Korff, Nest). Dharavi was once a fishing village that was incorporated into Bombay in 1872. It has excellent connections: highways run next to it, trains right through it and aeroplanes fly directly overhead, carrying shocked incoming tourists who look down upon it in dismay. But its connections are not restricted to transport. It exports products to the upper classes (who live in another world) as well as to several countries around the globe. Dharavi, and slums immediately adjacent, cover an area of only 200 hectares that together house a million inhabitants, more than two-thirds of whom actually work in the slum itself. In innumerable small workshops (or, more accurately, small-scale industries) they process leather, bone products and tendons for medicinal and musical use (arising from the original occupation of the first migrants who came in to do animal product processing) as well as ceramics, textiles, cane products and food. Pratima Panwalkar, social scientist, describes this place as the recycling capital of the country, where tons of plastic, paper, metal, glass and textiles are converted into raw materials or finished products. The fact that it is a consolidated slum with many houses built with permanent materials, with tarred roads, schools, chemists, police stations and a vocational college, and that its daily turnover exceeds €3 million a day cannot conceal the abject poverty, the dangerously unsanitary living and working conditions, and the appalling overcrowding. Its economic basis has become increasingly precarious since the politically provoked ethnic riots of 1993, which resulted in mutual killings between people who had lived cheek-by-jowl for years. Berliners may have finally got rid of their Wall, but the Dharavi residents of the Hindu neigbourhood of Palwadi and of the predominantly Muslim quarter of Nawabnagar have suddenly had the brilliant idea of putting up a wall between them. I suppose this, too, is some kind of technology transfer.

Bombay's bloody riots of 1992–93 are having repercussions long after on an even larger stage – the national government is being rocked eight years later by judicial investigations, Supreme Court rulings, demonstrations, resignations and arrests of top politicians accused of instigating them. Dharavi is a precursor of how the city as an entity is bound to undergo a sea change during the next few decades. The migrant population will form the majority in most major cities, which will lie in the developing world, with the inevitable consequence that they will also rule them by sheer electoral arithmetic in any remotely democratic set-up. Beyond that, we will be compelled to exchange our present image of the city itself, from one of café-lined boulevards with comforting old buildings or even skyscrapers, to one of a single-storeyed sprawl of huts stretching for tens of kilometres in every direction. That is going to be the typical, dominant embodiment of the city, not the Manhattan or Hong Kong skyline.

It is no longer enough to look at cities in a regional or national context, what counts is their integration in the international division of labour and their standing in the global pecking order. The irony lies in the fact that Dharavi, one of the main power bases for nationalist and chauvinist parties, is actually just as globalised as the cosmopolitan Bombay it apparently despises. Whether it is their export-oriented economies, cultural consumption (TV, films), or material consumption (consumerism), the difference between the two lies only in the details. The supposedly anti-internationalist activists who won political power have long become pragmatic, acting like any other city administration would do to attract foreign investment and even host Michael Jackson concerts. Globalisation is all-embracing. It is more difficult to escape its hug than to embrace it back.

The saving grace of Bombay is that even here money is not everything. For many, Bombay is the most enjoyable and exciting city in India, and certainly the only one with a life that extends beyond 8:00 p.m. Bombay is full of film gossip, reflected glamour and humour – one recent billboard went: "Success is relative – the more the success, the more the relatives!" It is one of the few cities on the subcontinent where public space is used in a universal manner – a legacy of its international connections. The Marine Drive beach along the entire centre of town is free, a place where even the poor and the burdened go to look at an infinite horizon and let their eyes rest. For a people living under such conditions of stress, it is surprising how considerate and helpful they usually are to their fellows. This is manifest not just on the streets and

LONDON

Decline is not a natural law – sometimes when you're on top, you stay there. London is the home of 'the mother of Parliaments', Amnesty International and rich banks, but Londoners have discarded their stuffiness and discovered public space, good food and architecture not just as enjoyable, but also as profitable. London is consolidating its position as a classic world city with a conscience.

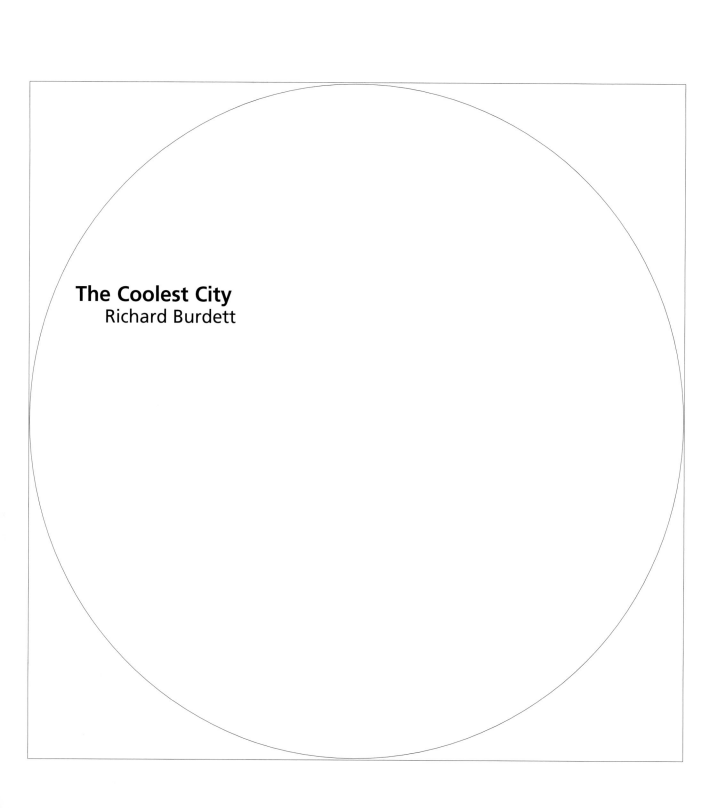

The Coolest City
Richard Burdett

LONDON

London, more than most cities, is susceptible to changes in the weather. Sunlight and the slightest hint of warmth bring an otherwise glum and grey city alive. Awkwardly, Londoners discover the pleasures of public life. They clamber out of their dark rooms, squinting at the intense light on their green parks and white-stuccoed terraces. In 2000, after the election of Ken Livingstone as the city's first ever directly elected mayor, London feels slightly different. It has moved a bit closer to achieving a more sunny disposition, one that is not totally dependent on the presence of the sun. But will it last?

Architecture, money and politics are the main generators of this new-found serenity. Over the last decade, the place has transformed itself. Not a carefully planned, top-down process of change but more of a D-I-Y revolution emerging from a combination of political, economic and cultural factors. Not all the changes result from the sea change impulses of Tony Blair's New Labour government. As we shall see, the seeds were, surprisingly enough, actually planted in the early 1990s during John Major's lame conservative government. Yet the Third Way (not capitalist, not socialist) government has been quick to claim ownership of London as the world's 'coolest city' – according to the authoritative international journal Newsweek. But is this a radical shift or simply an acceleration in the globalising process of this old world city? Has it rediscovered its role as mercantile capital with a conscience?

Halfway through the first year of the new millennium, London finds itself with a healthy economy and new public institutions. A new system of local government and an executive mayor are in place. As he walks into his office, Mayor Ken – as he wants to be called – has € 9 billion to spend. The effects of National Lottery cash are beginning to bear fruit with the opening of new museums, theatres and music halls. One million people have visited the new Tate Gallery (exhibiting high-culture) in six weeks while the Millennium Dome (displaying low-culture) struggles to meets its ambitious targets after the first six slow months.

A new underground line and an efficient rail link from Heathrow match the drama and speed of Channel Tunnel trains to Paris. New public monuments, from the Dome to the Millennium Wheel, mark the skyline while competing proposals for the world's tallest tower appear in the newspapers on a daily basis. And Londoners have discovered urban culture – from good coffee and toasted bagels at every street corner, strolling on the streets, to 24-hour shopping, bookstores and museums. The days when it was suspected that English women wore tweed underwear, and when it was known for certain that overboiled vegetables and greasy chips were considered 'food', are over.

You can smell the aroma of an Italian espresso or savour the self-satisfying taste of organic wheatgrass juice anywhere within a five-mile radius around Piccadilly Circus. The success of the cappuccino culture is such that central London authorities have a special squad to stop the encroachment of its pavements from bar tables and chairs. Railway stations and museum foyers are elegant, exciting places where you can sit and watch the world go by, no longer enveloped by that unique blend of English public squalor familiar from the past. Anyone who thinks that good cappuccino is not pertinent to urban culture doesn't remember what London streets or for that matter local coffee was like a couple of decades ago. Apart from baulking at the stratospheric cost of living, tourists enjoy London's new-found affair with public life. There is hardly a travel magazine that does not sing hymns to London's night life and food renaissance. Even the staid National Geographic recommends it enthusiastically as the place for young creative nonconformists to emigrate to.

The irony is that this success has been achieved during a period of maximum political fragmentation. London has not had a metropolitan government for the last 15 years, ever since the Greater London Council, the GLC, was abolished by Mrs. Thatcher for being cheeky. While the new mayor, Ken Livingstone, is the same person as the old leader of the GLC, things have changed. London's 33 municipal boroughs have developed a taste for political power and independence. New allegiances have been forged to promote single urban issues. While the economy has grown, deep divisions have been consolidated between rich and poor, East and West. The British capital still possesses some of the poorest urban areas in the whole of Europe. Youth unemployment and deprivation are highest in neighbourhoods with a high concentration of ethnic minorities and working classes. Public sector schools have deteriorated as dramatically as safety on the streets. The western corridor, opening out towards Heathrow airport, with good rail and road communications, continues to thrive with new business parks and corporate headquarters, skewing the distribution of jobs and wealth towards this side.

Increased wealth has generated a culture of individualism that transcends governments of the left or the right. The lack of affordable schools and public transport has pushed people out who cannot keep up with the galloping economic pace of the city. Yet it is one of the few cities in England that is witnessing a population gain. More people are moving in than moving out for the first time in 30 years. London, with its catchment area, the South-East of England, is one of the strongest economies in the western world. The region has a population of 15 million and a turnover equal to Denmark or Saudia Arabia. Only a quarter of the British population lives in South-East England, but 75% of the nation's wealth is created in this region. Following deregulation of the financial markets in the 1980s, the City of London, the small area that occupies the richest Square Mile in the world, has reinforced its classical position as a global financial centre together with New York and Tokyo, in spite of considerable efforts by rival cities, as Manuel Castells has illustrated.

London now has more corporate headquarters than any other world city, bringing global wealth and investment to the capital. Companies are still prepared to pay a premium for being in central London. It was recently voted the world's most popular business location despite its notorious cost of living. Ian Schrager, the American hotel king, has just opened two minimalist palaces, while Philippe Starck has completed a luxury design business hotel in the Canary Wharf office complex in the Docklands.

High-cost loft conversions, which cater to the transient international business community, accompany the expanding economy, creating new areas of gentrification in inner city zones close to the City. Clerkenwell, perfectly placed between central London and the City, has witnessed a proliferation of expensive residential conversions and bars that integrate successfully with the mixed social and economic grain of the area. Exmouth Market at the epicentre of Clerkenwell still services the Italian working class community, yet houses some of London's most trendy shops and restaurants. While gentrification is inevitably pushing up property values, the traditional working class communities who live in subsidised inner city accommodation are not under direct threat. It is the absence of affordable new housing and good inner city schools that are a problem in the growing economy, as is the miserable condition of the vast stock of public housing estates built in the 1950s and 1960s.

But while central government fiscal policy ensures that the Capital subsidises the poorer north of England, its boroughs are able to raise funds from local taxes, business rates, parking charges and licences The stronger the economy, the higher the tax revenue. The City of London borough council has one of the highest revenues in the world from the firms and banks located there, while having no money-swallowing institutions like schools and pensioner's homes. Westminster city council is not much different. The global reach of London's financial markets and its attraction as a place to live and do business continues to fuel the commercial property market until its next, inevitable, cycle of decline.

Despite the strength of its regional economy and growing tourist industry, the city is still affected by the cancer of social exclusion, unemployment and poverty. It is generating increased wealth on the basis of a lower employment base, causing increased differentials within the capital, particularly between the east and west of the city. Some of Europes' most deprived urban areas are in the south and east, even though average wealth – by comparison to other European cities – is high. After decades of decline, some of the central and inner areas are now showing an increase in population, fuelled by international migration. London has opened out, sucking in some of the best of Europe's younger generation. The notorious old Times headline, "Storm In Channel – Continent Isolated", no longer applies.

There has been significant inward migration from minority ethnic communities in boroughs such as Newham and Tower Hamlets in East London which almost doubled between 1981 and 1991. These changes have transformed the character of many inner city areas, bringing rich racial and cultural diversity as well as improvements to race relations in a traditionally chauvinistic society. The entire British establishment, including the monarchy, the government, the press and the churches, came out to condemn the isolated bomb attacks on minorities in 1998. Supported by a vibrant enterprise culture amongst the Asian community in particular, this social trend is driving urban regeneration. Philip Dodd, head of the Institute of Contemporary Arts, considers the second and third generations of Asians to be the city's leading cultural impulse, from music to street fashion, from new slang to video production, which all also happen to be high intensity economic activities.

The growth in financial services has attracts jobs and people from the continent, contributing to the cultural change in urban lifestyles extending from apartment and loft-living in the city centre to the greater enjoyment of street life, leisure and consumption of food. The restaurant scene is recognised as sophisticated and diverse, leading the designer and restaurateur Terence Conran to controversially claim London as 'the food capital of the world'. One can, arguably, eat better Indian food here than in restaurants in India, and fusion food has taken off to an amazing level of creativity and quality. Mayor Ken, who until recently was himself one of the capital's busy restaurant critics for the Evening Standard newspaper, will no doubt wish to encourage its culinary reputation, consolidating its position as a major international tourist location attracting over 25 million visitors a year.

The private sector is able to operate with relative freedom in the property market in spite of a relatively conservative planning framework. Extremely high business and residential rents make investment in property safe and attractive. The City of London is stuffed to the gills and companies are queuing up to find new premises. There is a surplus of demand over supply of modern offices. Hence the pressure for taller buildings, greater density and the search for new areas for commercial development – from Paddington in the west to London Bridge in the East. Meanwhile Canary Wharf in the Docklands is quietly doubling in size.

The Thames and the South Bank have been the focus of investment and change. The disappearance of the docks and its jobs in the 1970s created a vast area of social and physical deprivation along the entire length of the River Thames, eastwards towards the sea. Derelict riverside warehouses and vacant industrial land along the river provided the potential for redevelopment. When the economy picked up in the early 1990s and the demand for new housing and office space was high, developers pounced on these abandoned sites.

This is why the last remaining sites on the River Thames, close to public transport hubs and with enough space for large footprint buildings, are being snapped up for redevelopment. London Bridge City – a 20 acre site facing the Tower of London on the poorer South Bank which has been dormant for over 20 years - is now a € 1 billion commercial development. Only a small fragment will be occupied by Norman Foster's striking new offices for the Mayor and the Greater London Authority. This is a clever commercial operation – a privately built and owned City Hall – which matches current political aspirations for public-private partnerships, reflecting London's unique ability to balance these apparently conflicting interests.

This buoyant market has translated into new commissions for established design practices. Big money does not like taking big risks, especially in a culture that has historically not valued design. This is why the bulk of new commercial projects have gone to architectural practices known for their competence, delivery and reputation. The architecture offices of Foster, Rogers, Hopkins, Farrell and other established commercial firms like BDP, RMJM and EPR have grown exponentially in the last five years, with new buildings for Citibank, Hong Kong and Shanghai Bank, Daiwa and the many aggressive property developers. A big name not only impresses the board room but also guarantees credibility with the planning authorities. Emerging architects, however talented, still find it difficult to break into this market dominated by the hard pragmatics of cash flow, company profits and fast-track construction programmes.

On the residential side there is great pressure for growth. Government projections show that there is a requirement of about one million new households in the South East of England over the next 15 years. This is not due to population growth but to demographic change in British society: more divorcees and singles, people living longer and leaving home earlier. Many of these new households, nearly 80%, will be for single-person households rather than standard families with 2.4 children.

The impact of such large numbers on an already overcrowded country (England is the third most densely populated country after Bangladesh and Holland) prompted the government to look at the problem – and its opportunities – seriously. Last year it asked the architect Richard Rogers to assemble an Urban Task Force to investigate the causes of decline in English towns and to make practical recommendations to turn them round. Now that the Urban Task Force Report has been published, its recommendations are beginning to filter through to government policy. Most importantly, it is generating a cultural change in the public perception of design as a key player in urban regeneration. Central to this strategy of urban regeneration is the role of previously developed, so-called 'brownfield' land.

There are many brownfield sites – over 2000 hectares of disused railway yards, gas works and industrial areas – many of them along the Thames. There are also many vacant buildings – 20% of its housing stock is empty. The Urban Task Force has recommended that at least 60% of all new housing should be on central brownfield sites rather than greenfield sites outside city boundaries. It has also argued for higher density, well-designed and mixed-use environments as the way of promoting the revitalisation of inner city decline alongside jobs, better schools and social facilities.

The impact on the Urban Task Force on London could be significant. Rather than building more low-density, two-storey family houses – gated communities which have spread across the most prestigious locations for decades, especially in the Docklands – London is well-placed to support urban living. The Task Force message, strongly endorsed by the central government, is to encourage development in derelict areas which have good access to public transport. This is why the Jubilee Line Extension and the new high-speed rail connection to Stratford are so important.

Ralph Erskine's Greenwich Millennium Village, on the large contaminated Greenwich peninsula near the Millennium Dome designed by

Richard Rogers, is intended as an model of brown-field development. Despite its high political ambitions, this is a developer-led project funded by the private sector, which has benefited from substantial government investment in land reclamation and infrastructure. Close to the new Tube station at North Greenwich, a bus interchange designed by Norman Foster (notice how the same names crop up again and again?) and served by a new local transport system, the development has a radical approach to car parking and density. Only 75% of the units have parking spaces and the development density of 80 units per hectare is four times higher than the average for new housing.

The project for 1500 homes will deliver a much denser pattern of housing with a greater variety of units and tenures at a larger scale than we have seen in London for years. The Greenwich Millennium Village is being built around a school and health centre. Shops will be provided, but a large new "green" supermarket nearby will have an impact on the long-term viability of local retailers. Its claims for environmental and commercial sustainability will take time to implement, but the project constitutes a step-change from most developer-built housing. Prefabrication and flexible construction techniques, together with energy-saving and information technology provision in all units, will make a change to running costs and lifestyles. While first residents of the village will be living in a isolated neighbourhood, the long-term vision for a mixed urban community are positive and encouraging. The first units have been sold, suggesting that a more urban lifestyle that is not car-dependent is proving attractive to the indigenous population. While the Greenwich Millennium Village is neither revolutionary nor architecturally ground-breaking, as a residential development it represents an important model for urban regeneration in London.

England has lost an Empire, its superpower status and its manufacturing industry, but one thing it still owns is Time, if only because the International Meridian lies within it. Greenwich, of course, grabbed international attention at the centre of world time with its Millennium celebrations at the Dome and Greenwich Park. That is why the Millennium celebration was seen here as an important impulse for the construction of new landmarks. At least ten major projects which any other culture but the British would call 'grand' are complete. A new Opera House in Covent Garden and the Millennium Dome, the largest structure in the world, kicked off the year. Within a week in May 2000 the Queen has been busy opening three new projects – the grand Tate Modern Gallery in a disused power plant, the National Portrait Gallery and the Millennium Bridge. A long list of openings will keep her engaged for the rest of the year. Daniel Libeskind's Spiral at the Victoria and Albert Museum, Herzog and de Meuron Laban's Centre and more competitions for exciting new buildings at the South Bank Centre will keep the temperature high. Nearly all these projects have received at least 50% funding from the National Lottery, a creation of the last Conservative government.
Initially reviled by the churches as an expression of greed, the Lottery has become a kind of conscience, helping to realise projects for the public good. The bulk of the funds have been invested in capital projects for new arts and sports facilities, refurbishment of existing buildings and urban areas and special projects for the year 2000, all of which are projects traditionally difficult to get off the ground due to lack of finance. Despite regional jealousies, London has received no more than a fair proportion of the over € 4.5 billion in art galleries, museums, community centres and dance halls since 1996.

The effects of this extraordinary investment are suddenly emerging as a positive phenomenon in the life of the city. But while the cultural benefits to London are clear, the quality of the architecture of Lottery-funded projects has been uneven. This, to a degree is to be expected. Lottery projects receive funds on a competitive basis. Client groups (arts organisations, community groups, local authorities) commission designs, put together a business plan and then apply for money. Many of these clients groups have never managed, let alone procured million-pound buildings. Inevitably, problems have arisen between architect and client. It might have been expected that the Lottery would provide opportunities for the younger generation of architects. But the need to win a complex competitive bidding process, to raise matching funds, the general lack of design expertise amongst the new client bodies, and the very English concern with function and delivery have not worked in their favour. With few notable exceptions outside London – such as Caruso St John's excellent Walsall Art Gallery – the bulk of big Lottery projects has gone to big firms, adding to their healthy fee-income from the private sector. A list of major recipients of Lottery funds reads like a 'Who's Who' of the British architectural establishment with some notable exceptions such as David Chipperfield and Zaha Hadid, whose architecture is considered too adventurous for many public clients.

On the other side of the fence, a decision-making structure had to be invented overnight, one that was able to evaluate the commercial viability of the projects and their architectural quality. This has not been easy to achieve within a culture unused to investing public money on the basis of 'quality of design'. Yet, in their characteristic pragmatic efficient 'muddle through' way, the English have developed an mechanism that has delivered some outstanding results.

The Lottery has created a new generation of buildings in London which represents the architectural status quo: spanning from polite high-tech to well-mannered, cool modernism. Many projects are refurbishments of old buildings which limit the potential for architectural expression. Herzog & de Meuron's Tate Modern stands out as a major work which enriches the language in contemporary architecture in Britain. More modest in scale, Dixon.Jones' subtle intervention at the National Portrait Gallery, with its daylit court and superb views of Trafalgar Square, demonstrates the potential of a confident modern approach to revitalise a classical building. The Dome is a remarkable architectural and engineering structure in its own right, which signals the optimism and confidence of turn-of-the-century London. While some projects are struggling to survive, others are already embedded into the cultural life of the capital. The Serpentine Gallery in Hyde Park by John Miller, the National Maritime Museum and Dulwich Picture Gallery by Rick Mather and restored monuments including Somerset House and the Albert Memorial are enjoyed by locals and visitors alike.

It is not by chance that private sector know-how is being called in to manage and procure major cultural projects. The redevelopment of the South Bank Centre within Rick Mather's subtle new masterplan is being masterminded by one of London's most shrewd property tycoons, Elliott Bernerd, whose company is building the largest shopping centre in London and many office developments. Stanhope, the developers who broke new ground in London's office market in the 1980s with the Broadgate development, are behind the implementation of the Tate Gallery and Covent Garden Opera House. Stuart Lipton, chief executive of Stanhope, has recently been put in charge of government architectural policy at the head of the new Commission of Architecture and the Built Environment.

Apart from its effect on the cityscape, one of the main effects of National Lottery funds has been the enormous leverage of public and private funds that would not normally have been channelled into public and arts buildings. The Tate's € 98 million Lottery grant brought in a further € 60 million from the public sector and € 98 million from private donations. Similar sums have been achieved on other key projects. London has become more American-like in fundraising style, using the Lottery cash as a lever to raise matching funds.

Potentially the most dramatic and vibrant spatial experiences are to be found below ground. The eleven new stations of the Jubilee Line Extension have been forcefully masterminded by Roland Paoletti, the chief architect of the project. They are, in effect, pure architectural statements, unaffected by the aesthetic conventions that constrain the design of buildings above ground. The Tube stations represent a true cross-section of the eclectic state of British architecture today – from Foster and Wilkinson's rigorous steel-and-glass language to MacCormac and Alsop's evocative experimentations with space, colour, materials and light. Whereas sceptics dispute the positive effects or even the popularity of these quality projects among the poorer sections of the population, they fail to point out the inevitable results of the alternative, namely, of nothing happening, of no change at all, of stagnation.

Initiated by the Thatcher government in the late 1980s to help Canary Wharf, the Jubilee Line Extension will do more to transform the poorer regions in the city's South and East than any amount of government or EU investment. Its realisation reflects London's age-old compromise between the needs of capital and the political aspirations of the time. It is no accident that Livingstone's successful main election platform was the improvement and retention of the Tube in public hands. For more than a century, South London has been poorly served by underground lines because of adverse geological conditions in the flood plain of the Thames. New tunnelling techniques have allowed the construction of the new line which crosses the river three times in its journey from central London to Stratford, connecting new poles of activity in Canary Wharf and Greenwich with still derelict urban areas around Bermondsey, West Ham and Newham. Its destination in Stratford coincides with the terminus of the high-speed rail link currently under construction to the Channel Tunnel. When complete in 2007, Stratford will replace Waterloo Station as the arrival point for visitors from the Continent, helping to regenerate one of the largest deprived urban areas in Europe.

Mayor Ken will be experiencing a sense of *déjà-vu*. His first words as Mayor were, "It's good to be back!" But the structure of London politics has been radically overhauled. Instead of a large, bureaucratic but politically friendly GLC which used to appoint its chairman, he will have to deal with the lean and divided Greater London Authority – a 25-person committee whose remit is to watch over him; and with local authorities and agencies which have become used to fighting their own corner. Some – like the right-wing City of Westminster, the maverick Borough of Southwark and the cash-rich City of London – have relished their independence.

Poorer boroughs have made a virtue of necessity and used their status as underdogs to stimulate change and investment. Southwark and Greenwich, for example, have been proactive in attracting government, EU and Lottery funds to their areas – highlighting urban deprivation and chronic under-investment. Much effort has gone into building a legacy from these projects, to secure lasting investment for deprived ethnic minorities, schools and social institutions.

New allegiances have been forged to promote single urban issues. The Cross-River Partnership broke new ground in metropolitan politics by bringing together the central London riparian boroughs of different political colour to bid for funds and co-ordinate riverside projects including new bridges, the Millennium Wheel, and improved walkways. It has been extremely successful, as one can see from the intensity of activity if one walks from Westminster to London Bridge. London First, another self-generated group representing business interests in the capital, has successfully campaigned for environmental and transport initiatives. Public debates organised by initiatives like London Open House and the Architecture Foundation have attracted thousands of participants. Over the last 15 years, though, planning decisions have been taken by local political committees, reflecting local concerns and priorities. For this reason many difficult sites, especially those cutting across political boundaries, have been left untouched. Norman Foster's ambitious plans to pedestrianise part of the Trafalgar Square were blocked by the City of Westminster even though they would positively affect the capital of the nation as a whole, because they go against the interests of a few influential local residents.

The Mayor's strongest card will be to pull rank on those areas that cut across local authority boundaries and to formalise what has happened as a result of these ad-hoc alliances. First will be a joint development strategy for London's big 'holes' – starting from that vast area of inner city dereliction that stretches for fifteen kilometres on both sides of the river – the East Thames Gateway.

In 2000, London has no strategic plan. There is no metropolitan-wide policy which determines where new housing, shops, leisure or offices should go. Despite the high level of building activity along the Thames, there is no strategy for the great river. The London Planning Advisory Committee (LPAC) has been just that: an advisory body, not an executive one. Clearly, the Mayor and his team will change this to a degree.

Mayor Ken will need to address wider issues. He is directly accountable to five million voters, one of the largest political constituencies in Europe. He will want to be re-elected in five years time. New projects, new jobs and new houses will be popular initiatives which attract votes. He will have powers to stop cars from entering central London by introducing 'congestion charges'. He will be able to funnel public and private funds into a better public transport system, improving links to areas in the east and to the south of the city. Most importantly, the Mayor will be able to balance the boom-and-bust cycle of the market-driven property sector with public investment in projects and infrastructure. This is why there is cause for optimism for the future of this great city.

But London has always had a structural distaste for 'grand plans' and top-down intervention. It has a unique organic morphology. It is a collection of villages rather than a walled capital. Unlike Paris, Berlin or Vienna, it has never yielded to formal urban plans, not even after the Great Fire of London in 1666. There have been individual urban set-pieces of great architectural value – from Nash' Regent Street to the great Victorian Improvements. But London resists order imposed from above. Tony Blair's inability to control the election – Mayor Ken is an independent, not a Labour man any more – reflects a cultural condition that transcends politics.

So, even though London feels different now, at a profound level it is much the same. It has always been and remains a city that responds to the needs of commerce and capital, recognising the political and social potential of a world city. Architecture and the built environment will continue to play a major role. The architectural historian John Summerson described 18th century English town-planning tradition as "quintessentially pragmatic…a coincidence of intent and circumstance." Two centuries later, London displays the same robust characteristics of expediency enhanced with a strong social and an increasingly cultural conscience, with a will to keep it that way.

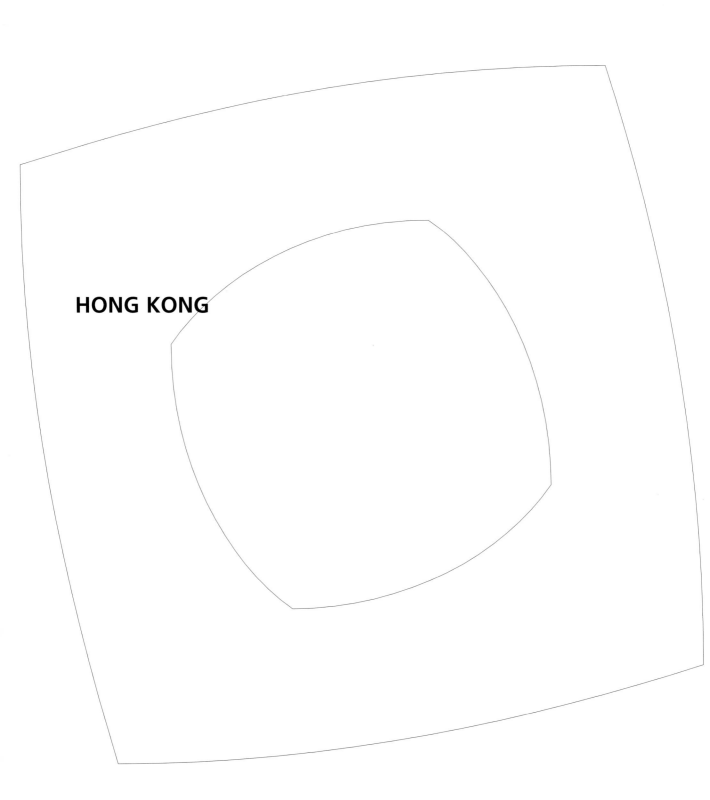

HONG KONG

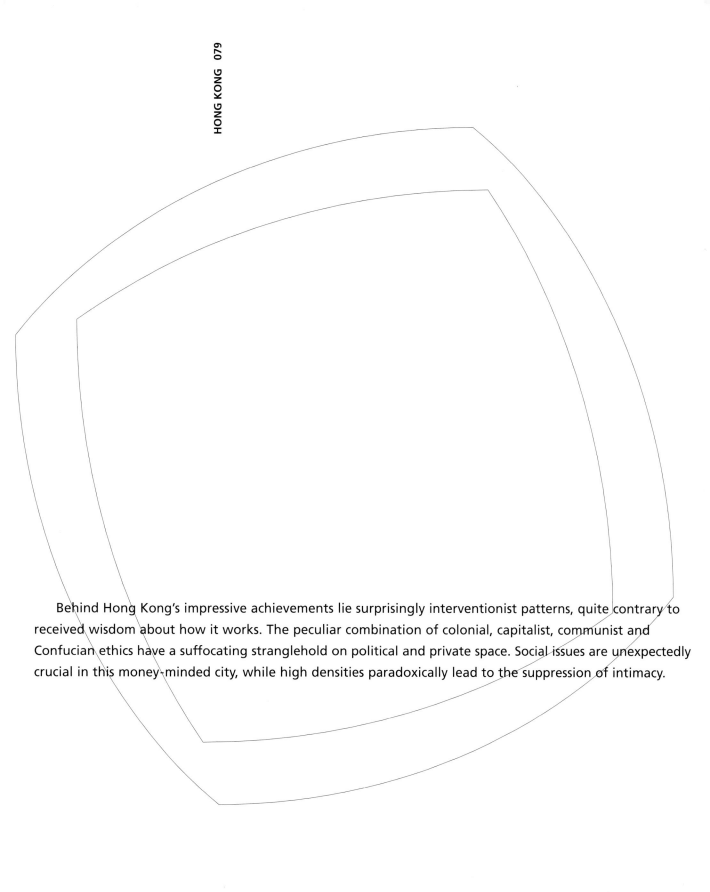

Behind Hong Kong's impressive achievements lie surprisingly interventionist patterns, quite contrary to received wisdom about how it works. The peculiar combination of colonial, capitalist, communist and Confucian ethics have a suffocating stranglehold on political and private space. Social issues are unexpectedly crucial in this money-minded city, while high densities paradoxically lead to the suppression of intimacy.

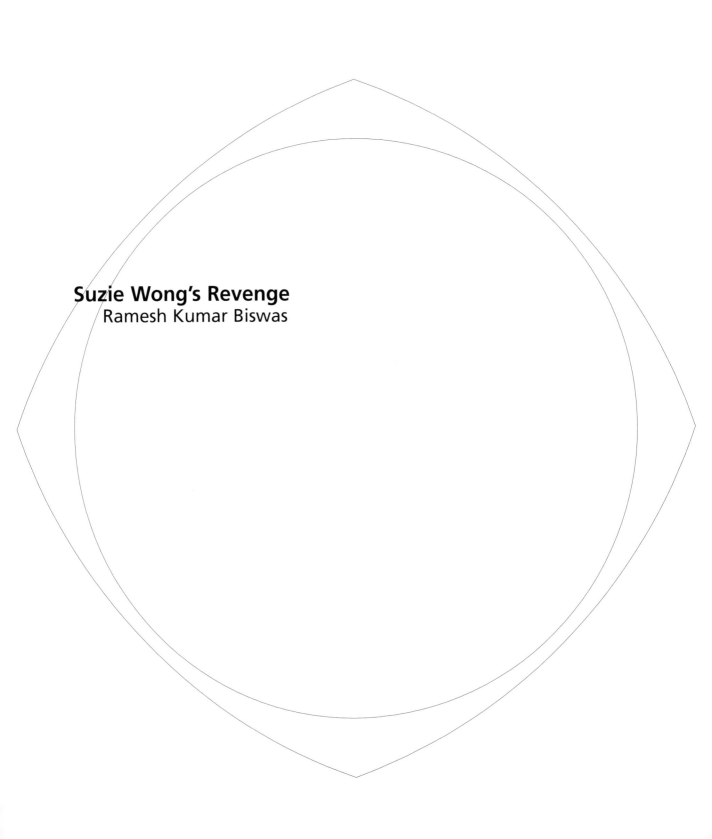

Suzie Wong's Revenge
Ramesh Kumar Biswas

HONG KONG

During a stay in Hong Kong some years ago I was shown a curious item in the newspaper: a burglar, interrupted on the job while breaking into a jewellery shop, was chased through Hong Kong in a dramatic scene akin to those often seen in local film productions. When he was finally caught, police confiscated the plastic bag with his loot and were astonished to find no jewellery in it, but instead two *feng shui* fish swimming around in water. Speculation was rife that the thief had stolen them out of personal animosity, in order to expose their owner to evil powers.

Another 'man on the run', the hero of the hit movie "The Odd One Dies" directed by Patrick Yau, could be seen as the typical Hong Kong citizen, himself a refugee or descended from refugees, occasionally returning to Hong Kong on a foreign passport after a further flight to America or Australia, ready to leave again any day. These are the people who have made Hong Kong what it is, from William Jardine to the latest refugee: restless and ruthless people full of strong ambition and business instinct. Even journalists who descend upon Hong Kong like birds of prey on two-day missions seem to be men on the run. Hardly a *cliché* has ever been spared: pictures of the spectacular harbour full of picturesque junks and of luxurious villas on the peak, tales of the only pure market economy without any limitations or rules, of decadent quarters of leisure, of the noble British and the bad, bad Chinese. Many visitors to Hong Kong appear to have an imaginary mental construct of the city. They do not let reality get in the way. But like many *clichés*, even these contain a grain of truth. The dynamics of this city, however, are more complex: neither do the supposed pleasure-loving nature of the residents or their leanings towards sexual excesses hold water, nor do the supposedly free-market mechanisms accord with misleading first impressions.

Hong Kong has reached the omega-point in the intensivity of urban life, as the urban planner Alexander Cuthbert, formerly of Hong Kong University, has written. It is without a doubt one of the great world cities, but he is disturbed by the absence of any of the characteristics usually associated with world cities of this size and importance. There are no beautiful squares, parks or boulevards, hardly any grandiose public, religious or cultural buildings, not even any pleasant residential quarters. History is being systematically eradicated in this city, buildings appear to be being pulled down almost as soon as they are finished, to be replaced by yet taller ones, making it a permanently noisy building site. Fast. Dense. Smoky. A place that, as Cuthbert remarks, "seems to demand humans without fixed dimensions, in order to squeeze them into ever smaller cubes. But why should we judge all cities with the same measure? Why should European or even Indian urban design principles be valid for a city whose population is more than 80 percent Chinese? Would that not be arrogant? When the shape of a city is a result of its social order, would it not be logical to assume that the structure of this massively Chinese influenced city is one that is formed and willed by its residents? This assumption would, however, totally ignore the influence of British imperialism and the modern global economy on the urban development of Hong Kong. Furthermore, one finds hardly any visible traces of Chinese aesthetic, cultural, architectonic or urban design traditions here. It would then be just as arrogant to take for granted that the Chinese love to live in congested cages perched on top of each other. Chinese immigrants in Canada or Australia prefer to live in large rather than in tiny houses (as demonstrated by their "monster houses" in Montreal). Hong Kong is in truth not a Chinese city, but a capitalist city."

He claims that there is no evident will to city-building, that the form of the city is more of a by-product of immigration and economic activity. This means that any production of social space in the city is accidental and has little to do with architectonic principles of form or imagination. The *genius loci* is that of commodity space that dominates building activity and suppresses popular culture. The complex synergies of social, economic and cultural factors that make a city have been reduced primarily to one activity, namely that of the exchange of goods. According to Cuthbert's analysis, this monofunctional space is steadily moving away from worth for the user towards exchange value, from social cohesion to alienation.

Nevertheless, almost every visitor to Hong Kong leaves with deep impressions of a lively, vibrating, fascinating big city. "The location", as architecture critics tend to say when they do not want to hurt anybody by expressing anything negative about the building itself, "the location is truly spectacular".

But the chance to build a city of beauty and dignity on this unique landscape has been lost. "Too late for the City-State, a topographic marvel, an architectural hodgepodge", moans the writer Jan Morris. It is not the physical city that so fascinates but the interplay of two different cultures: Victorian colonialism and Confucian pragmatism, sometimes opposed, sometimes amazingly similar, that shaped a particular brand of capitalism, alternating layers at varied levels of everyday life – with all its movement and variety – whose complex patterns are so direct and powerful. The shaping of private space, the emergence of a particular private life and of a suppressed erotic sphere, are all consequences of this specific situation. These deeply entrenched structures are now being rapidly overlaid by the Mainland agenda.

Yes, it is an incredibly invigorating city, but let's not leave it at that. Everyone seems to recognise in Hong Kong whatever they wanted to see in the first place. Daily news journalists are not the only ones to have been blinded by the propaganda. Milton Friedman, guru of monetarism, also chose the interpretation that suited his creed: "We may well ask if there exist any contemporaneous examples of societies that rely primarily on voluntary exchange through the market to organise their economic activity and in which the government is limited…perhaps the best example is Hong Kong… It has no tariffs or other restraints on international trade…It has no government direction of economic activity, no minimum wage laws, no fixing of prices…Government plays an important but limited role…It reinforces law and order, provides a means for formulating the rules of conduct, adjudicates disputes, facilitates transportation and communication and supervises the issuance of currency…If you want to see how capitalism really works, take a look at Hong Kong." The arch-conservative Heritage Foundation in the US and the Wall Street Journal have both claimed that, "In Hong Kong, the government does not interfere in the marketplace", this in 1996, at a time when one should have long been aware of the complexity of the internal relationships, the interventionist role of the colonial state and its growing contradictions, as well as of the extensive subsidies to capital. More serious studies ('The Hong Kong Model' by Schiffer; 'The Sek Kip Mei Syndrome: Economic Development and Public Housing in Hong Kong and Singapore', by Castells, Goh & Kwok; the HK issue of the journal Cultural Studies); or even the mainstream, simplified weekly prayer book for managers, 'The Economist' out of London, have finally cleared such myths about the "Hong Kong Miracle".

It is correct to state that the government does not openly interfere in economic activity, but both State intervention and steering through indirect transactions and subsidies, and the personal overlaps between administration and business are open for anyone to see, not hidden as elsewhere. The low level of interference by the Crown in the years before 1997 has led some to talk of "pseudo-colonialism", but that would be to show a naïve ignorance of deep-rooted colonial structures still in operation, even if now manned by local Chinese. Hong Kong is actually very 'scrutable' (to coin a phrase, since the only inscrutable face I ever saw there was that of a fried snake once served to me). In the *de facto* cabinet that governed the Crown Colony, the Executive Councillors were nominated by banks, property developers, insurance companies and trading houses, while high bureaucrats occupied lucrative second jobs in the boards of big firms. Mercenary mandarins were part of the corporate state. 65% of the members of the parliament, the Legislative Council, were company representatives, even after the half-hearted, self-serving reforms of the last Governor, who managed to introduce a sort of election for 43% of the seats. Paradoxically, the old system fits in almost seamlessly into the new: these structures have not changed in practice noticeably since the takeover, though the atmosphere is not quite as cosy. The Beijing-appointed Chief Executive of the SAR (Special Administrative Region) Government, who was re-elected in mid-2000 by an Election Committee mostly made up of representatives of major companies, which, in turn, are controlled by a few families; as well as many of his administration's members at various levels are multi-millionaire businessmen. The bureaucracy is still deeply involved in raising fiscal revenue through exchange transactions primarily in connection with land and building permits. State interference has become even more direct (e.g., in 1998 the SAR government bought up large numbers of blue-chip stocks to counteract foreign speculation and to end the plummeting fall of the stock market. They were then released to the public in the fall of 1999 in the form of closed-end

'HKtrack' mutual funds, the unit price of which subsequently skyrocketed).

There is no doubt that Hong Kong is one of the most successful regions in the world. With barely 7 million residents in uninterrupted activity it exports more goods than the whole of China or the whole of India (1.2 and one billion residents respectively). Its efficiency and pace are legendary. The initial hiccups with luggage and cargo sorting when the new Chek Lap Kok Airport started up only made the evening news on TV worldwide because it had happened in Hong Kong. Frankly, if the same situation had cropped up in Dhaka or Athens, would you have even noticed? Admiration for its striking achievements should not prevent us from looking at the system more closely. We discover that assets and investments need not be declared here, direct taxes are low or non-existent, but high indirect taxes in connection with land transactions compensate for this. The superficial observer might perceive the busy harbour of Hong Kong, with its hundreds of cargo ships, tankers, junks, houseboats and brightly lit floating restaurants as the city's most important element, even its *raison d'etre.*

Wrong again! What is coveted most in this city full of people who have never had property or have lost everything is: land, land and land again. Land scarcity has dimensions beyond the real, geographic difficulties of terrain. Property ownership is almost an obsession amongst refugees – after all, this city's population consists almost exclusively of refugees and their descendants.

Land was also used by their ruler, the Crown, as its central budget mechanism. Although, of course, state-owned land and buildings have also ameliorated overcrowding and insanitary conditions at crucial moments of mass immigration to the island, they were primarily instrumentalised to contribute to the economy. The ability to raise more than a third of state revenue through land leases, more than non-taxation sources contribute in any other capitalist country, makes the government the most important player in economic growth and a major form-giver to the city. The 70% drop in tourism and retail revenue and the significant rise in unemployment due to the Asian crisis and the return to China has not only forced Hong Kong's shopkeepers to be unexpectedly polite, but has also animated the government to use land to crank up investment. Gigantic projects such as the Western Rail Link from Lantau to the Mainland with a handful of new towns along the way are being initiated by the HK administration, steps quite contrary to the standard prescriptions of the IMF and the illusions of monetarists of the likes of Friedman & Co.

Anyone who has left the glittering shopping centres to walk around in the high-rise housing districts may well ask: How has so much activity, money, opportunity and energy resulted in such a thoroughly degraded urban environment? Solely economic interpretations will have to be enhanced by a look at the interplay of three power dimensions and their influence on spatial structure: a state without broad democratic legitimacy, big capital and the traditional clan network. The illusion of an ideology-free system of the rule of law under British sovereignty guaranteeing justice and the common good crumbles after a more exact analysis of past lobbying in law making, conflicts within the different value systems and interest groups, frequent bending of laws, cronyism and plain cheating. Joseph Cheng of the City University of Hong Kong sees the recent increase in the number of public protests and in support for the opposition as an indicator of greater pressures, inequalities and unfairness in the distribution of resources, and of wider public rejection of the stubborn structures behind it. I believe it is also a manifestation of the general rise in understanding of political and economic mechanisms in the wake of the Asian crisis.

Like a married couple which papers over its conflicts in the interests of the family, the intertwining of the imperial and local systems is mutually supporting and is evident even in the city map. Cuthbert notes that monumental neo-classical symbols of dignified imperial institutions – trading houses, banks, courts, government offices, shipping companies – were set up along the main streets in the Central district. Running at right angles to them were narrow streets full of three-storey tenements and noisy, smelly street markets. That is, the lines in one direction of the urban grid revealed a function of early capitalism (centralised, hierarchical, rigid, conservative, rule-ridden), whereas the lines in the other direction of the grid represented the activities of an early market economy (multi-polar, decentral, spontaneous, flexible, network-like).

Cuthbert's analysis is that this differentiation has been successively erased, so that today nothing stands in the way of the merging of brutal Hong Kong capitalism with what could be called the Market Stalinism of the adjoining South Chinese regions. In this scenario, also analysed by economic sociologist Jeffrey Henderson, the norms of company law would be retained to protect joint ventures, while workers' and individual rights would be decimated to match the disappearing importance of the citizen, and to speed up his 'abolition' as a subject. In spite of the differences and open mistrust between the parties, the upper strata have developed an arrangement in the air space between London, Beijing, the Hong Kong Government and its business community. While Hong Kong-style aesthetics and business are permeating Chinese cities, China-style politics is taking over Hong Kong, as recent conflicts involving restrictions on the independence of professions, the reunion of families and the scope of tolerated political engagement demonstrate. Though only two uniformed Red Army guards are visible in the whole city, outside their garrison, it would be naïve to overlook the influence that Beijing has gained (by the way, a 1969 dictionary interestingly defines naïve as "lack of urbanity").

Earlier, the entry of unskilled labour after World War II and the Bretton Woods agreement gave rise to demands for major changes in the city structure. The move from the exchange to the production of wares led to alterations in the system of production, transport and consumption as well as massive state intervention to reduce costs for industry. Since land was one of the main sources of revenue, an artificial scarcity was introduced in spite of (or perhaps due to) the fact that according to the Treaty between China and Britain, the colonial government was not permitted to sell land until 1997, only to lease it (in China itself there is still no private ownership of urban land). A look at the map of HK, or a glance out of the window of a plane approaching it, reveals an astonishing amount of green land, of which only small parcels are gradually released by the government for extremely high-density and high-rise development in order to keep up prices. A pleasant side-effect of this policy is that one can leave the city (though not the crowds) and be in idyllic woods within half an hour – there is none of the endless urban sprawl typical of other megacities. But Hong Kong would not be Hong Kong if this impression of careful land management, too, was not a mistaken one. The 'ecological footprint' of Hong Kong actually extends far into the South China cities of the Pearl River Delta, where it is strikingly wasteful of land and resources as well as being dangerously polluting. In spite of high prices and high densities, new housing developments are oversubscribed up to 40 times. Families camp outside developers' offices overnight on the day of issue as if it were the first day of the Knightsbridge summer sales. Flats then change hands up to 15 times during construction, adding to the price every time right up till completion. Urban planning is used as a social instrument: functional plans divide work, social reproduction and retail areas, atomising the city further. It angers one to see that so little of the city is influenced by the people who live here. At the same time the liberalisation of building heights, the reclamation of land, and the introduction of multi-storey factories, vertical versions of Engels' Manchester, went hand-in-hand with the reduction of complexity in the built environment. A residential tower, a factory tower or an office tower can only be differentiated by the signs on them: "Plum Sauce Condominiums","T-Shirts with Various Labels", "Trading in Stocks and Securities" (or was it "Shocks and Insecurities"?).

Feverish attempts are being made to replace land as main revenue source by communications technologies, and there are some success stories here: a HK-owned British telecom company, Orange, has profited hugely from its takeover deal with Mannesmann. The restructuring of the world economy is mirrored in the dialectics between economic and spatial transformation. Hong Kong's growth as an entrepot to China and the entire South East Asian region in the fields of financial services and information technologies has led to an endlessly rising demand from finance capital for locations in central areas. There is no end to the number of towers built for banks, corporations, hotels and luxury apartments: nodes for worldwide communication networks, they have very little to do with the street in which they stand. This has a devastating effect on the public use of the urban matrix.

I would not attempt to deny anyone a certain fascination for this irresistible show of dynamics and this merciless force of activity in the pursuit of money. But not to recognise the raw brutality and destructive consequences of this development results in a patronising but fatal naïvety similar to that of George Bernard Shaw, who after visiting the Soviet Union in the 1920s declared, "I have seen the future, and it works".

The paternalist role of the government does not extend significantly to public amenities. Other cities may fail to provide them, but this one does not even try very hard. Since the city is unwilling to renounce its revenues from land transactions and equally unwilling to pay the high prices that it itself determines for land, it does not fulfil even its own embarrassingly low standards for public space. To make up for this, the business sector is compelled to participate in a typical trade-off mechanism – private developers who provide public spaces are allowed to build even higher than usual. The resulting hotel lobbies, shopping centres and skywalks above street level are accessible to all and are striking for their apparent generosity. However, many of them only have limited access – they are closed at night and during certain festivities or holidays, when entrance fees are suddenly introduced. The streets have been surrendered to the automobile. Police, security personnel and a veritable phalanx of video cameras regulate access, use and behaviour. Security criteria, not civitas and urban life, are in the foreground, even during the planning phase. This development is not unintentional. Even leisure is seen as a ware, with a profit line at the end of the bill. In this system, merely walking around, relaxing and enjoying oneself without buying anything is considered a pure waste of time. The residents of Hong Kong have been so intensively injected with Calvinist and Confucian work ethics, that they consider just doing nothing strange – perhaps even enviable, but unaffordable.

The few cultural facilities that do exist in the city are under-utilised. The yellow-tiled "Cultural Centre", an ingenious building directly on the waterfront with spectacular views of the harbour if only they hadn't forgotten the windows, is usually empty. When I visited the new City Aquarium, I was surrounded by families discussing suitable recipes for the exotic sea life on show. The elegant new Convention Centre on the other side of the harbour, built for the handover, is used more often for trade fairs than for cultural events.

The most striking illustration of this attitude is public response to the use of the free space beneath architect Norman Foster's spectacular Hong Kong and Shanghai Bank headquarters building. Connecting two of the most expensive business streets in Central, this non-commercial space at street level, an incredible gesture to the city for whatever actual reason, has become practically the sole postmodern public space on the island. For the good citizens of Hong Kong, deprived of free communal facilities for decades, a space which does not make money is inexplicable. Sunday upon Sunday, as has been often described by astounded observers, the Philippine community meets here to exchange news and read out letters from home, sing songs on the guitar, grill fish *al fresco*, to dance and generally enjoy themselves. (Filipinos have been working here since the middle of the 19th century, but the city obviously hasn't had sufficient time to accept them as human beings – a well-known beeper-service brochure offers a value-added item, a device to be fitted on to your television set to alert you in your office when – I quote – "your Filipino maid switches on the TV"). Most of them maids and nurses who work under subhuman conditions, they come out on their only free day. From the very early hours they stream from the Star Ferry terminal, a swelling sea of people and voices. The proper upper-classes, for whom parties, receptions and social occasions are rarely pure pleasure and are usually connected to business, are irritated by such spontaneity and fun. After several unsuccessful attempts to ban this scandalous weekly event, the unambiguous "better" burgher of Hong Kong is now reduced to venting his spleen in regular letters to the editor. A further thorn in the side was the extraterritorial Walled City of Kowloon, a rare example of an anarchist city within the city, with all its positive and negative facets. This self-governing settlement, which kept the Hong Kong administration from its gates until China lifted its protection in 1992, was systematically evacuated with the helping hand of armed police, carefully scoured and disinfected from top to bottom, and then: dynamited. Some form of exorcism? Very thorough, anyway.

The massive environmental degradation of potential public space and the step-by-step privatisation of leisure continue to limit the possibilities that residents have as political citizens. The concept of public space has been perverted to such an extent that its use for civil society is almost unthinkable, ironically at a point in the city's history when more HK residents than ever before are engaged with human rights, environmental and political activism. The earlier paternal view, that people who have escaped political persecution are happy to live without politics as long as they can make money, was belied by the results of local elections, at which the opposition has won all the freely elected seats.

Can the combined deprivation of both public and private space be pure coincidence? Private space is – what a paradox in this supposed paradise of neo-liberal self-realisation – just as subtly manipulated by the system as public space. Again we have an unexpected meeting of minds, of the colonial administration and the Confucian social system. A look at the chronicles show us that the city had an advanced urban infrastructure at the turn of the last century: post offices, trams, street lighting and sewers were installed at the same time as in major cities in the West. Between the 1911 revolution on the mainland and the beginning of the Sino-Japanese War the population increased by more than one million. At the end of that war it rose to one and a half million, which means that it had tripled within three decades. But all such data reveal nothing about the real living conditions of the people. The free influx of people dramatically worsened conditions. The official living area per person was fixed at 2.2 square metres per person. After 1937 the administration could not even implement this minimum rule. In 1936 there were 9.9 persons per residential unit, in 1939 the average rose to 17.4, and in the poorer areas to an unbelievable 55 persons per unit – this according to official figures.

At the time only private speculative developers were building in Kowloon. The rigid, stratified Victorian colonial hierarchy was housed after a suitable manner on the Peak of Victoria Island, where higher officials and rich businessmen lived, other than the Chinese, of course. The expression "Peak mentality" described the world view of officials whose knowledge of local conditions was gained from a height of 400 metres above sea level. Down below the population had reached 1.9 million by 1940, a half million of whom slept in the streets. In 1941 Japan conquered the Crown Colony. The city emptied as rapidly as it had filled up before. When the Second World War ended there were only 500 000 people left, many of them British prisoners of war in concentration camps. As the Red Army occupied the major cities on the Mainland in 1949, the population rose to more than a million. Once again there was a drastic increase in the number of people per residential unit, namely 21.4. The wave of refugees from China kept up until the 60s: the Census of 1961 spoke of 3.1 million of whom a million were homeless: 511 000 slept in temporary structures, 140 000 people shared beds in shifts, 69 000 slept on verandas, 56 000 on roofs, 56 000 in garages and stairways, 26 000 in boats, 20 000 on the street, 12 000 further down in cellars and a further 10 000 even deeper down, in caves – altogether a quarter of the urban population. Indescribable as living conditions were for these people, those who lived in official housing were not much better off. The poisoning of Nature and the destabilisation of social structures had seriously begun. This led even the arch-capitalists and officials of both ethnic groups to the insight that a modern industrial state could not flourish for any length of time with its workers living in such miserable conditions; even if only due to the risk of epidemics or civil uprising. A solution had to be found that would not cost the business community anything but (rather practical idea), if possible, bring in some money to them.

The refugees were not only penniless farmers and workers. A few industrialists from Shanghai had begun to move their capital and machinery systematically to Hong Kong for some time before the Revolution, as S.L. Wong chronicles in his book "Emigrant Entrepreneurs". Very quickly refugee capital and refugee labour, together with the latest textile machinery from Britain, created the basis for the industrialisation of the Colony, which remains even today the world's biggest clothing exporter, though no longer a major producer. The small size of firms allowed the continuation of essentially pre-capitalist, authoritarian forms of management and production. At this point a fascinating and complex symbiosis of the ruling and money-making classes of both cultures took place. Behind the facade of paternal capitalism Hong Kong has developed an almost incomparable welfare system, a central element of its spectacular economic success.

This supposedly laissez-faire regime directs over 40% of public expenditure to social services, a stunning proportion in any context, surpassing that of the 'welfare states' of Europe. This money was also used to realise the public housing programme that now houses about 48% of the total population, that is, about 85% of the employed. This impressive statistic is hidden in the latest issue of "HK Background Facts", published annually by the Government Information Services, as if it was something to be ashamed of, between more important valiant deeds such as Major Container Port, New Airport, Western Harbour Crossing, West Kowloon Expressway, Lantau Bridge Link and so forth. The process was first speeded up by the establishment of the HK Housing Society in 1951, the HK Housing Authority in 1954 and the 1964 White Paper that planned the construction of 1.9 million units – with an average living area of 3.25 sq m in social housing or 2.23 sq m in relocation projects – within ten years, a goal that was later increased. The emergence of this, the world's proportionately biggest public housing programme after Singapore, was partly an answer to the crisis of legitimacy of the colonial state. Public political mobilisation, especially anti-colonial unrest in 1966 – 67, demanded an active counter-strategy. The state had to re-establish its existence on the basis of a new social contract with numerous social forces to save its colonial skin and its autocratic form. The massive housing programme is also a product of internal economic policy and the peculiar relationship to land ownership for a capitalist country, as sociologists J. Henderson and S.K. Lau have described. State land and social housing resulted in de facto subsidies of labour costs through lower taxation and the freeing of capital for investment. This enormous effort has, like most of the colonial State's policies, been almost exclusively to the benefit of employers.

Even this programme has not been left untouched by the change of regime: the new Chief Executive's 1997 plan to build 85 000 new units has been casually shelved because of the 50% drop in real estate prices, in spite of the public and media uproar. And, of course, many other activities are being superannuated by the rapid emergence of new factors and new ways of making money. These changes are apparently being seen by citizens as detrimental to their welfare and their standard of living – witness the first ever massive demonstrations by civil servants in mid – 2000, and an end – 2000 survey that shows 59% of Hong Kongers are less satisfied with the new regime than with the old one. It is not, therefore, my case that all the old structures are still dominant – after all, the last years of the Crown administration were not particularly Victorian in style, and high-flying HK entrepreneurs between Beijing and London are not visibly driven by either Confucius or Mao. But the underlying, innate historic and cultural currents cannot be refuted.

It is not easy to envy the tenants of these Lego-block housing schemes, where the density reaches a giddy 150 000 persons per sq km. If Berlin were to be filled with the same density within its present limits, 80 million people would be living there – the entire population of Germany. In principle, high densities are preferable to urban sprawl due to the savings in infrastructure costs and land use, and desirable for the potential they might offer in terms of enhanced public facilities and services. However, Hong Kong has only saved on the one, without offering the other. It has been said that only multi-millionaires and the homeless live on ground level.

The rest are stuffed into housing blocks, 35 to 50 storeys high, many still offering the old standard of only 3.25 sq m per person, raised in some new buildings to 5.5 sq m per head. Some time ago I read in the papers about an extremely rich dealer in aphrodisiacs (for some inexplicable reason a highly lucrative profession) who had been murdered by the Triads in his 100 sq m flat. A rather small flat for such a wealthy person, which he even shared with his two grown-up sons and their families. On the average, the happy family that now moves into a 40 sq m flat in a relocation area would consist of at least eight members.

One does not need an exceptionally wild imagination to picture the social and sexual restrictions of such a situation. Once again Victorian/Calvinist prudery plus work ethic meets Confucian asceticism plus (take a guess) work ethic. Work and the welfare of the family are valued more than individual needs. Flats for workers are primarily meant to be sleeping stations – any extra space for any kind of personal, exuberant sensual enjoyment would be at the cost of efficiency and would inevitably interfere with productivity. Time, energy and concentration are to be directed to work and yet more work. No private pleasure, except during the Chinese New Year holiday, when shutters come down and large quantities of mind-numbing *mao tai* are consumed around *mah jongg* tables. The tiny flats are not just a by-product of the high-price policy for building land, but also, according to sociologists D.K.L. Ho and Rance Lee from the Chinese University of HK, a conscious strategy to define narrow limits to the private sphere – especially the sex life and the reproductive rate of the workers. Outrageous as such as assumption might seem at first glance, one doesn't have to believe in any conspiracy theory to note certain systematic recurring patterns. The government has refused to finance scientific studies about the effects of extremely highly population density and housing form on human sexuality. The socially and sexually repressive housing policy is full of scurrilous aspects.

Every day, when ferries dock at the island of Lantau in the bay, old women flock to them brandishing photos of rooms with large beds to be rented by the hour to young student couples or office workers who, lacking their own rooms, come here to enjoy secret love – or even absolutely legal marital love. Even that which is taken for granted elsewhere must be bought and paid for in Hong Kong.

Hong Kong is lascivious only to the superficial observer. Sociologists consider it one of most sexually repressed places on earth. True, there is constant gossip about sexual scandals and forbidden liaisons, about police lists of prominent homosexuals and secret brothels, not surprising in a city which long had a gender ratio of five men to one woman (lucky woman? poor woman?). This commercialisation of sex continued during the Korean and Vietnam 'police actions', during which the Wanchai district became an "R&R" zone for the U.S. Army. The "World of Suzie Wong" (a novel about a Wanchai prostitute with a heart of gold) became a phrase indelibly associated with the city, to the evident irritation of present officials of the Government Information Services. Perhaps the pleasureless nature of this area is the revenge of the repressed and the sexually exploited. For, as Jan Morris remarks, this red light district (with hotel signs saying "Rooms Purely To Let"), has a peculiarly artificial aspect to it, an empty, calculated and purchasable nature typical of the sterile pleasures of this city – an impression reinforced by the panoply of neon advertising signs which, due to the central downtown airport and busy sea traffic navigation, were forced by law to be still, not to blink or to jump around cheekily Las Vegas style, but to remain petrified, like unblinking eyes. Now that the airport has moved out of the sitting room, now that the neon signs blink, now that the crisis has forced it to paddle even faster, now that it is in a limbo between two systems, Hong Kong is busy discovering new insecurities, new directions and new energies.

A city has an invisible, almost personal, intimate history which reveals itself after much searching, a story transcending the hard facts of economics and politics, a history which is on the run even as it is perceived. The filling of private space with sensual spirits cannot be smothered even in the most blatantly money-driven surroundings. Blake's 'London' goes: "How the youthful harlot's curse/ Blasts the new-born infant's tear...". Can we begin, perhaps in Hong Kong, to look for a dimension beyond urban architectures and economic structures – towards an *erotics* of the city?

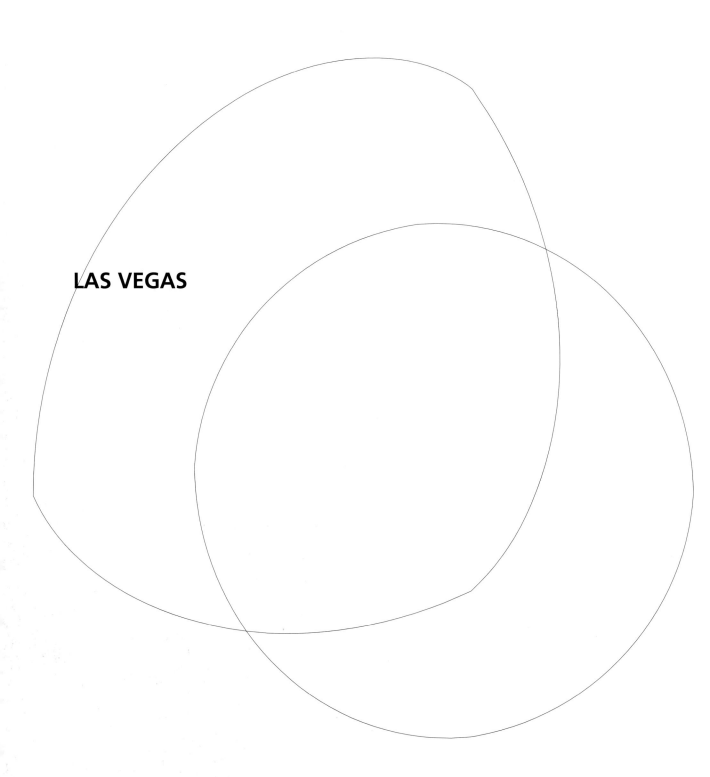

LAS VEGAS

Exceeding Mecca in numbers as a place of pilgrimage, this neon city encapsulates much that has gone wrong in American urban development. Billions of dollars of voluntary 'idiot's tax' are paid annually by gamblers to finance a place of concentrated absurdities and bad taste, at constant war with the environment.

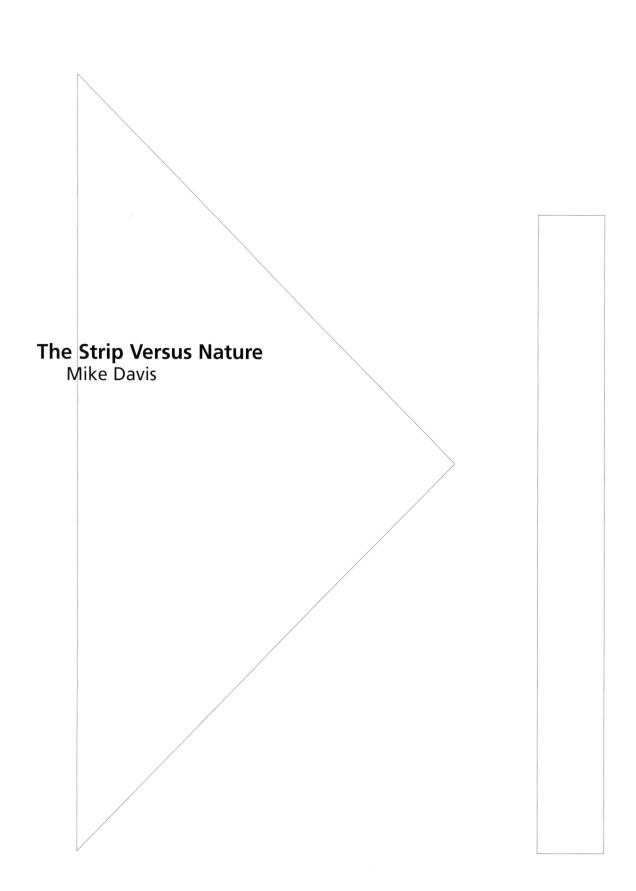

The Strip Versus Nature
Mike Davis

It was advertised as the biggest non-nuclear explosion in Nevada's history. On October 27, 1993, Steve Wynn, the state's official "god of hospitality," flashed his trademark smile and pushed the detonator button. As 200 000 Las Vegans cheered, the Dunes Hotel, former flagship of the Strip, slowly crumbled to the desert floor. The giant dust plume was visible from the California border. Nobody in Nevada found it the least bit strange that Wynn's gift to the city he adores was to blow up an important piece of its past. This was simply urban renewal Vegas-style: one costly façade destroyed to make way for another. Indeed, the destruction of the Dunes merely encouraged other casino owners to blow up their obsolete properties with equal fanfare: the Sands, of Rat Pack fame, came down in November 1996, while the Hacienda was dynamited at the stroke of midnight that New Year's Eve. Extravagant demolitions have become Las Vegas's version of civic festivals.

LAS VEGAS

In place of the old Dunes, the Mirage Resort is completing the €1.25 billion Bellagio, a super-resort with lakes large enough for jet-skiing. No one bothered to explain where the water would come from. Neither did those who built the €2 billion, 6000-room Venetian Casino Resort, with gondolas along artificial canals; nor has Circus Enterprises, which is transforming the old Hacienda into Project Paradise, "an ancient forbidden city on a lush tropical island with Hawaiian-style waves and a swim-up shark exhibit." €8 billion has been invested in thirteen major properties along the Strip alone. As a result, the Sphinx now shares a street address with the Statue of Liberty, the Eiffel Tower, Treasure Island, the Land of Oz and the Piazza San Marco. The boom, still breaking all records, shows every sign of continuing.

By obscure coincidence, the demolition of the Dunes happened on the centenary of Frederick J. Turner's legendary "end of the frontier" address to the World's Exposition in Chicago, where the young prairie historian ruminated on the fate of American character in a conquered, rapidly urbani-sing West. Turner questioned the survival of frontier democracy in the emergent epoch of giant cities and wondered what the West would be like a century hence.

The robber barons of the Strip think they know the answer: Las Vegas is the terminus of Western history, the end of the trail. As an overpowering cultural artefact it bestrides the gateway to the twenty-first century in the same way that Burnham's 'White City' along the Chicago lakefront was supposed to prefigure the 20th. At the edge of the millennium, this strange amalgam of boomtown, world's fair and highway robbery is the fastest growing metropolitan area in the US. It is also the brightest star in the neon firmament of postmodernism.

More than 32 million tourists had their pockets picked by its one-arm bandits in 1999: a staggering 33 percent increase since 1990. (By the time you read this, Vegas should be hard on the heels of Orlando, Florida, the world's premiere tourist destination with 35 million visitors to Disney World, Universal- and MGM Studios;). While southern California has suffered its worst recession since the 30s, Las Vegas has generated tens of thousands of new jobs in construction, gaming and security services. As a consequence nearly a thousand new residents, half of them Californians, arrive each week. Some of the immigrants are downwardly mobile blue-collar families seeking a new start in the Vegas boom. Others are affluent retirees headed for a gated suburb in what they imagine is a golden sanctuary from urban turmoil. Increasing numbers are young Latinos, the new sinews of the casino-and-hotel economy. In spring 1995, Clark County's population passed the one million mark, and anxious demographers predicted that it will grow by another million before 2010.

This explosive growth has dramatically accelerated the environmental deterioration of the American Southwest. Las Vegas long ago outstripped its own natural-resource infrastructure, and its ecological "footprint" now covers southern Nevada, parts of California and Arizona. The hydrofetishism of Wynn (he once proposed turning downtown's Fremont Street into a pseudo-Venetian Grand Canal) sets the standard for the Las Vegan's profligate overconsumption of water: 1800 litres daily per capita versus 1055 in Los Angeles, 800 in Tucson, and 550 in Oakland. In a desert basin that receives only 10 cm of annual rainfall (less than 30 percent of L.A.'s precipitation), irrigation of lawns and golf courses (60 percent of Las Vegas's total water consumption) – not to mention artificial lakes and lagoons – adds the equivalent of another 50 to 75 cm of rainfall.

Yet southern Nevada has little water capital to squander. As Johnny-come-lately to the Colorado Basin water wars, it has to sip Lake Mead through the smallest straw. At the same time, reckless groundwater overdrafts in the Valley are producing widespread subsidence of the city's foundations. The Strip is several metres lower today than in 1960, and some subdivisions have had to be abandoned.

Natural aridity dictates a fastidiously conservative water ethic. But Las Vegas haughtily disdains to live within its means. Instead, it is aggressively turning its profligacy into environmental terrorism against its neighbours. "Give us your water, or we will die," developers demand of politicians grown fat on campaign contributions from the gaming industry. Las Vegas is currently pursuing two long-term, fundamentally imperialist strategies for expanding its water resources.

First, the SN Water Authority is threatening to divert water from the Virgin River or steal it from ranchers in sparsely populated central Nevada. In 1989 the Authority stunned rural Nevadans by filing claims on more than 800 000 units of surface and groundwater rights. This infamous water grab ("cooperative water project" in official parlance) brought together an unprecedented coalition of rural Nevadans against it: ranchers, miners, farmers, the Moapa Band of Paiutes and environmentalists. Their battle cry has been "Remember Owens Valley," in reference to L.A.'s notorious annexation of water rights in the once-lush valley in the Sierra Nevada: an act of environmental piracy immortalised in the film 'Chinatown'. Angry residents of Owens Valley blew up the L.A. Aqueduct during the 1920s, and some central Nevadans have threatened to do the same to any pipeline hijacking local water to Las Vegas. Las Vegas and the Los Angeles area want to divert the allocation of Colorado River water away from agriculture and toward their respective metropolitan regions.

Finally, to return to yet another 'Chinatown' parallel, watchdog groups such as the Nevada Seniors Coalition and the Sierra Club are increasingly concerned that the Water Authority's €1.7 billion delivery system from Lake Mead may be irrigating huge speculative real-estate profits along metropolitan Las Vegas's undeveloped edge. One major pipeline runs near the suburb of Henderson where private investors recently acquired huge parcels in a complicated land swap with the Bureau of Land Management, which controls most of the desert periphery. This is the same equation – undervalued land plus publicly subsidised water – that made instant millions for an 'inside syndicate' when the L.A. Aqueduct was brought to the arid San Fernando Valley in 1913.

Southern Nevada is as thirsty for fossil fuels as it is for water. Tourists naturally imagine that the world's most famous nocturnal light show is plugged directly into the turbines of nearby Hoover Dam. In fact, most of the dam's output is exported to California. Electricity for the Strip, as well as for the two million lights of the new and dis-concerting "Fremont Street Experience", is provided by coal-burning and pollution-spewing plants on the Moapa Indian Reservation and along the Colorado River. Only 4% of Las Vegas's current electricity comes from "clean" hydropower. Cheap power for the gaming industry, moreover, is directly subsidised by higher rates for residential consumers.

Automobiles, of course, are the other side of the fossil fuel prob-lem. As Clark County's transportation director testified in 1996, the county has the "lowest vehicle occupancy rate in the country" in tan-dem with the "longest per person, per trip, per day ratio". Like Phoenix and Los Angeles before it, Las Vegas was once a Mecca for those seek-ing the restorative powers of pure desert air. Now, according to the Environmental Protection Agency, Las Vegas has supplanted New York as the city with the fifth highest number of days with "unhealthy air" Its smog already contributes to the ochre shroud over the Grand Canyon and is also reducing visibility in California's East Mojave National Recreation Area.

Las Vegas, moreover, is a major base camp for the panzer divisions of motorised toys – dune buggies, dirt bikes, speed boats, jet-skis – that make war each weekend on the fragile desert environment. Few west-ern landscapes are more degraded than the lower Colorado River Valley, which is under relentless attack by the leisure classes.

Skyscraper casinos and luxury condos share the west bank with the mega-polluting Mojave Power Plant, which devours coal slurry pumped with water stolen from Hopi mesas hundreds of miles to the east. Directly across the river, sprawling and violent Mohave County, Arizona provides trailer-park housing for the non-union, minimum-wage work-force, as well as a breeding ground for antigovernment militias à la McVeigh. The Las Vegas "miracle" demonstrates the fanatical persistence of an environmentally and socially bankrupt system of human settle-ment and confirms Edward Abbey's worst nightmares about the emergence of an apocalyptic urbanism. Although post-modern philosophers (who don't have to live there) delight in the Strip's "virtuality" or "hyperreality", most of Clark County is stamped from a monotonously real and familiar mould. Las Vegas, in essence, is a hyperbolic L.A. – the Land of Sunshine on fast-forward.

The historical template for all low-density, resource-intensive southwestern cities was the great expansion of the 1929s that brought two million midwesterners and their automobiles to L.A. County. This was the "Ur" boom that defined the Sunbelt. Despite the warnings of an entire generation of planners and environmentalists, regional planning and open-space conservation again fell by the wayside during the post–1945 population explosion. In a famous article for 'Fortune' in 1958, sociologist William Whyte described (flying from Los Angeles to San Bernardino) "an unnerving lesson in man's infinite capacity to mess up his environment – the traveller can see a legion of bulldozers gnawing into the last remaining tract of green between two cities". He baptised this insidious growth-form "urban sprawl".

Although Las Vegas's third-generation sprawl incorporates some innovations (casino-anchored shopping centres, for example), it otherwise recapitulates with robot-like fidelity the seven deadly sins of L.A. and its Sunbelt clones such as Phoenix and Orange County. Las Vegas has
1 abdicated a responsible water ethic;
2 fragmented local government and subordinated it to private corporate planning;
3 produced a negligible amount of useable public space;
4 abjured the use of "hazard zoning" to mitigate natural disaster and conserve landscape;
5 dispersed land uses over an enormous, unnecessary area;
6 embraced the resulting dictatorship of the automobile; and
7 tolerated extreme social and racial inequality.

Why all this talk about water? In 'mediterranean' California or the desert Southwest, water use is the most obvious measure of the environmental efficiency of the built environment. Accepting the constraint of local watersheds and groundwater reservoirs is a powerful stimulus to good urban design. It focuses social ingenuity on problems of resource conservation, fosters more compact and efficient settlement patterns, and generates respect for the native landscape. In a nutshell, it makes for "smart" urbanism, as seen in modern Israel or the classical city-states of Andalucia and the Maghreb, with a bias toward continual economies in resource consumption.

Southern California in the early Citrus era, when water recycling was at a premium, was a laboratory of environmental innovation, as evinced by such inventions as solar heating (widespread until the 1920s) and state-of-the-art wastewater recovery technologies. Its departure from the path of water rectitude, and thus smart urbanism, began with the Owens Valley aqueduct and culminated in the 1940s with the arrival of federally subsidised water from the Colorado River. Hoover Dam extended the suburban frontier deep into California's basins and underpriced traditional conservation practices such as sewer-farming and stormwater recovery out of existence.

Unlike L.A., Las Vegas has never practised environmental conservation or design on any large scale. It was born dumb. Cheap water has allowed it to exorcise even the most residual semiotic allusion to its roots. Visitors to the Strip, with its tropical islands and Manhattan skylines, will search in vain for any reference to the Wild West (whether dude ranches or raunchy saloons) that themed the first-generation casinos of the Bugsy Siegel era. The desert has lost all positive presence as landscape or habitat; it is merely the dark, brooding backdrop for the neon Babel. Profligacy likewise dissolves many of the traditional bonds of common citizenship. L.A. County is notorious for its profusion of special-interest governments – "phantom cities," "county islands," and tax shelters – all designed to concentrate land use and fiscal powers in the hands of special interests. Clark County, however, manages to exceed even L.A. in its radical dilution and dispersal of public authority.

The city limits encompass barely one-third of the metropolitan population (versus nearly half in L.A.). The major regional assets – the Strip, the Convention Center, McCarran Airport and the University of Nevada – are located in an unincorporated township aptly named Paradise, while poverty, unemployment and homelessness are disproportionately concentrated within the boundaries of the cities of Las Vegas and North Las Vegas. This is a political geography diabolically conceived to separate tax resources from regional social needs. Huge, sprawling county electoral districts weaken the power of minorities and working-class voters. Un-incorporation, conversely, centralises land-use decision making in the hands of an invisible government of gaming corporations and giant developers. In particular, the billion-dollar corporate investments along the Strip – with their huge social costs in terms of congestion, water and power consumption, housing and schools – force the fiscally malnourished public sector to play constant catch-up. This structural power asymmetry between the gaming corporations and local government is most dramatically expressed in the financing of new public infrastructure to accommodate casino and tourism expansion. Contrary to neo-classical economic dogmas and trendy "public choice" theory, corporate-controlled economic development within a marketplace of weak, competing local governments is inherently inefficient. Consider the enormous empty lots in the urbanised fabric of Las Vegas, dramatically visible from the air, that epitomise the leapfrog pattern of development that planners have denounced in California because it unnecessarily raises the costs of streets, utilities and schools. Crucial habitat for humans as well as for endangered species, in the form of parks, is destroyed for the sake of vacant lots and suburban desolation.

Similarly, both L.A. and Las Vegas zealously cultivate the image of infinite opportunity for fun in the sun. In reality, however, free recreation is more accessible in older eastern and mid-western cities that cherish their parks and public landscapes. Although the beach crisis was partially ameliorated in the 1950s, L.A. remains the most park-poor of major American cities, with only one-third of the useable per capita open space of New York City.

Las Vegas has virtually no commons at all: just a skinflint 0.7 hectares per thousand residents, compared with the national minimum of 4.05 hectares. This park shortage may mean little to the tourist jet-skiing across Lake Mead or lounging by the pool, but it defines a impoverished quality of life for low-wage service workers who live in the stucco tenements that line the side streets of the Strip. Boosters' claims about hundreds of thousands of acres of choice recreational land in Clark County refer to car-trip destinations, not open space within walking distance of homes and schools. One is not a substitute for the other.

Some of the most beautiful desert areas near Las Vegas are now imperiled by rampant urbanisation. Developers are attempting to raise land values by privatising natural amenities as landscape capital. The Sierra Club has recently mobilised against Summerlin West, a segment of the giant planned community that is the chief legacy of Howard Hughes, upon Red Rock Canyon – native Las Vegans' favourite site for weekend hikes and picnics. The project, as endorsed by the Las Vegas City Council (which was subsequently allowed to annex the development), encompasses 20 000 homes, two casinos, five golf courses and nearly 600 000 sq m of office and commercial space. As one local paper put it, most environmental activists were "less than enthused about the possibility of lining one end of Red Rock Canyon, one of the valley's most pristine landmarks, with casinos, businesses and homes."

The recreation crisis in Sunbelt cities, of course, is the flip side of the failure to preserve native ecosystems, another consequence of which is the loss of protection from natural hazards such as floods and fires. The linkage between these issues is part of a lost legacy of urban environmentalism espoused by planners and landscape architects during the City Beautiful era. In 1930 the city designer Frederick Olmsted, Jr. recommended "hazard zoning" to L.A. County as the best strategy for reducing the social costs of inevitable floods, wildfires and earthquakes. In this sadly unrealised vision, development would have been prohibited in floodplains and fire-prone foothills. These terrains were best suited for preservation as multipurpose greenbelts and wilderness parks, with the specific goal of increasing outdoor recreational opportunities for poorer citizens.

Las Vegas is everything Olmsted abhorred. Its artificial deserts of concrete and asphalt have greatly exacerbated its summer flash-flood problem (probably the city's best-kept secret, except on occasions, as in 1992, when unsuspecting tourists drown in casino parking lots). L.A. was the first world metropolis to be decisively shaped in the era of its greatest growth by the automobile. One result was the decentralisation of shopping and culture and the steady atrophy of its downtown district. A group at the University of California at Irvine have suggested that we are seeing in Orange County and other edge cities "the birth of a post-suburban metropolis" where traditional central-place functions (culture and sports, government, high-end shopping, and corporate administration) are radically dispersed among scattered locations. Whether or not this is a general tendency, contemporary Las Vegas recapitulates Orange County in an extreme form. The gaming industry has displaced most other civic activities from the centre to the periphery. Tourism and poverty now occupy the core of the metropolis. Other traditional downtown features, such as shopping areas, cultural complexes and business headquarters, are chaotically strewn across Las Vegas Valley with the apparent logic of a plane wreck.

Meanwhile its booming suburbs stubbornly reject physical and social integration. To use the nomenclature of 'Blade Runner', they are self-contained "off-worlds," prizing their security and social exclusivity above all else. Planning historian William Fulton has recently described suburban Las Vegas as a "back to the future" version of 1950s southern California: "it is no wonder that the L.A. homebuilders love Las Vegas. Not only can they tap into a L.A.-style market with L.A.-style products, but they can do things the way they used to do them in the good old days in L.A." As Fulton points out, while California homebuilders must now pay part of the costs of the new schools and services, Vegas developers "pay absolutely no fees toward new infrastructure."

The most ambitious of Las Vegas's "off Worlds" is Summerlin. It boasts of complete self-sufficiency (it's "a world within itself," according to one billboard) with its own shopping centres, golf courses, hospitals, retirement community and (what else) casinos. "Our goal is a total community," explains president Mark Fine, "with a master plan embracing a unique lifestyle where one can live, work and play in a safe and aesthetic environment." Residents rather than corporations pay for key infrastructure such as the new expressway. When Summerlin is completed, a population of more than 200000 living in 26 income- and age-differentiated "villages" will be hermetically sealed in Las Vegas's own up-scale version of Arizona's leaky Biosphere.

The formerly gritty mill town of Henderson has also become a major growth pole for walled, middle-income subdivisions. It may soon surpass Reno as Nevada's second-largest city. For optimal advantage in its tax obligations, Summerlin is divided between the city of Las Vegas and unincorporated Clark County. On the edge of Henderson is the larval Xanadu of Lake Las Vegas: a fantasy created by erecting an eighteen-story dam across Las Vegas Wash. "The largest privately funded development under construction in North America," according to a brochure, Lake Las Vegas is sheer hyperbole, including €2 million lakefront villas in a gated subdivision within a larger guard-gated residential community. The grand plan envisions the construction of six major resorts anchored by luxury hotels and casinos, as well as five golf courses in addition to "restaurant and retail shops that will be the upscale alternative for Las Vegas."

Las Vegas's centrifugal urban structure reinforces a slavish dependence upon the automobile. According to formerly trendy architectural theorists such as Robert Venturi and Denise Scott Brown, whose 'Learning from Las Vegas' has been a founding text of postmodernism, Las Vegas Boulevard is supposed to be the apotheosis of car-defined urbanism, the mother of strips. Yet the boom of the last decade has made the Strip itself almost impassable. The Boulevard is usually as gridlocked as the San Diego Freeway at rush hour and its intersection with Tropicana is supposedly the busiest street corner in the nation.

As a result frustrated tourists soon discover that the ride from McCarran Airport (immediately adjacent to the Strip) to their hotel frequently takes longer than the plane flight from L.A. The Brobdingnagian scale of the properties and the savage summer heat, not to mention the constant assault by hawkers of sex-for-sale broadsheets, can turn pedestrian expeditions into ordeals for the elderly and families with children. The absence of coherent planning for the Strip as a whole (the inescapable consequence of giving the gaming corporations total control over the development of their sites) has led to a series of desperate, patchwork solutions, including a few new pedestrian overpasses. The Nevada Resort Association – representing the major gaming corporations – is relying on new freeways to divert cross-traffic from the Strip and a proposed €1.2 billion monorail to speed customers between the casino-hotels.

Thus contemporary Las Vegas is one vast freeway construction site. Nothing has been learned from the dismal California experience, not even the elementary lesson that freeways increase sprawl and thus the demand for more freeways. When completed, the new Las Vegas freeway network will allow most local commuters to bypass the Strip entirely, but it will also centrifuge population growth further into the desert, with correspondingly high costs for infrastructure and schools.

One index of the extraordinary power wielded by the resort association is the fact that the relative contribution of gaming taxes to state revenue actually declined during the 'annus mirabilis' of 1995 when hotel-casino construction broke all records. Yet the industry, shaken by riots in 1992, is not unconscious that eroding education and social services will eventually produce social pathologies that may undermine the city's resort atmosphere. Their ingenious solution after months of top-level discussion in 1997 has been to volunteer the room tax increase – which is directly passed on to tourists and then spent exclusively on the Strip monorail – as a "heroic" act of social responsibility. This reduced the tax heat on the casino owners while conveying the clear message, scripted by resort association lobbyists, that the time had come for homebuilders and small-business owners to make a contribution to school finance. In the meantime, hypergrowth without counterpart social spending has increased economic inequality. Despite the feverish boom, the supply of jobless immigrants has far outpaced the demand for new workers in the unionised core of the gaming economy. The difference translates into a growing population of marginal workers trapped in minimum-wage service jobs, the non-union gaming sector, and sex and drug economies. According to one estimate, the homeless population increased 750 percent during the superheated boom years of 1990 – 1995. A larger percentage of residents lack health insurance than the inhabitants of any other major city. It is plagued by soaring rates of violent crime, child abuse, mental illness, lung cancer, epidemic illness, suicide, and – what no one wants to talk about – a compulsive gambling problem that is a major factor in family pathologies.

This obviously provides a poor setting for the assimilation of Las Vegas's new ethnic and racial diversity. Despite consent decrees and strong support for affirmative action from the Culinary Workers Union, the gaming industry remains far from achieving racial or gender equality. In the past, Las Vegas more than earned its reputation as "Mississippi West." While African-American entertainers such as Sammy Davis Jr. and Nat King Cole were capitalising the Strip with their talent, blacks were barred from most hotels and casinos, except as maids, through the 1960s. Indeed, a comparative study during that period of residential discrimination across the United States found that Las Vegas was the "most segregated city in the nation." More recently, high unemployment rates in the predominantly black Westside precipitated four violent weekends of rioting in 1992. Interethnic tensions have also increased as Latinos have replaced African-Americans as the largest minority group.

Let's return to Las Vegas and the end of western history. In his apocalyptic potboiler, 'The Stand' (1992), Stephen King envisioned Las Vegas as Satan's earthly capital, with the Evil One enthroned in the MGM Grand. Environmentalists, together with the imperilled small-town populations of Las Vegas' desert hinterlands, would probably agree with this characterisation of the Glitterdome's diabolical 'zeitgeist'. No other city in the West seems to be as driven by occult forces or as unresponsive to social or natural constraints. Like its parent L.A., Las Vegas seems headed for some kind of eschatological crack-up (in the King novel, Satan ultimately nukes himself).

Confronted with the Devil himself and his inexorable plan for two-million-plus Las Vegans, what can the community do? Environmentalists can either continue to defend natural resources and areas one at a time against the juggernaut of development: a purely defensive course that may win individual victories but is guaranteed to lose the larger war. On the other hand, they can oppose development at the source by fighting for a moratorium on further population growth in the arid Southwest. Pursued abstractly, however, this dogmatic option will only pigeonhole Greens as enemies of jobs and labour unions. Indeed some environmentalists may even lose themselves in the Malthusian blind alley of border control, by allying themselves with nativist groups that want to deport hardworking Latino immigrants whose per capita consumption of resources is only a small fraction of that of their native-born employers.

A better approach, even if utopian in the short-run, would focus comprehensively on the character of desert urbanisation. "Carrying capacity" is not just a linear function of population and available resource base; it is also determined by the social form of consumption, and that is ultimately a question of urban design. Cities have incredible, if largely untapped, capacities for the efficient use of scarce natural resources. Above all, they have the potential to counterpose public affluence (great libraries, parks, museums and so on) as a real alternative to privatised consumerism and thus cut through the apparent contradiction between improving standards of living and accepting the limits imposed by ecosystems and finite natural resources.

In this perspective, the most damning indictment against the Sunbelt city is the atrophy of classical urban and pro-environmental qualities such as residential density, pedestrian scale, mass transit, and a wealth of public landscapes. Instead, L.A. and its postmodern clones are stupefied by the ready availability of artificially cheap water, power and land. Bad design has unforeseen environmental consequences, as illustrated by southern Nevada's colossal consumption of electric power. Instead of mitigating its desert climate through creative design (proper orientation of buildings, maximum use of shade, minimisation of heat-absorbing "hardscape", short distances and so on), Las Vegas simply relies on universal air-conditioning. But, thanks to the law of conservation of energy, the waste heat is merely exported into the general environment. As a result, Las Vegas is a scorching "heat island" whose nightly temperatures are frequently 10 degrees hotter than the surrounding desert.

Fortunately, embattled environmentalists have some new allies – inner-city residents, senior citizens, advocates of children, environmentalists – all of whom are fundamentally disadvantaged by the suburban, automobile-dominated city. The New Urbanism has had many successes in California, the Pacific Northwest and other areas where preservation of environmental quality commands a majority electoral constituency. In the Southwest, by contrast, the Summerlin model – with its extreme segregation of land uses and income groups, as well as its slavish dependence upon cheap water and energy – remains the "best practice" standard of the building industry. The New Urbanism by itself is a starting point, not a panacea. A Green politics for the urban desert would equally have to assimilate and synthesise decades of international research on human habitats in dryland environments. It would also have to consider alternatives to a regional economy that has become fatally dependent upon a casino-theme park monoculture. Creating a vision of an alternative, sustainable and democratic urbanism in the Southwest is an extraordinary challenge. But this may be the last generation even given the opportunity to try.

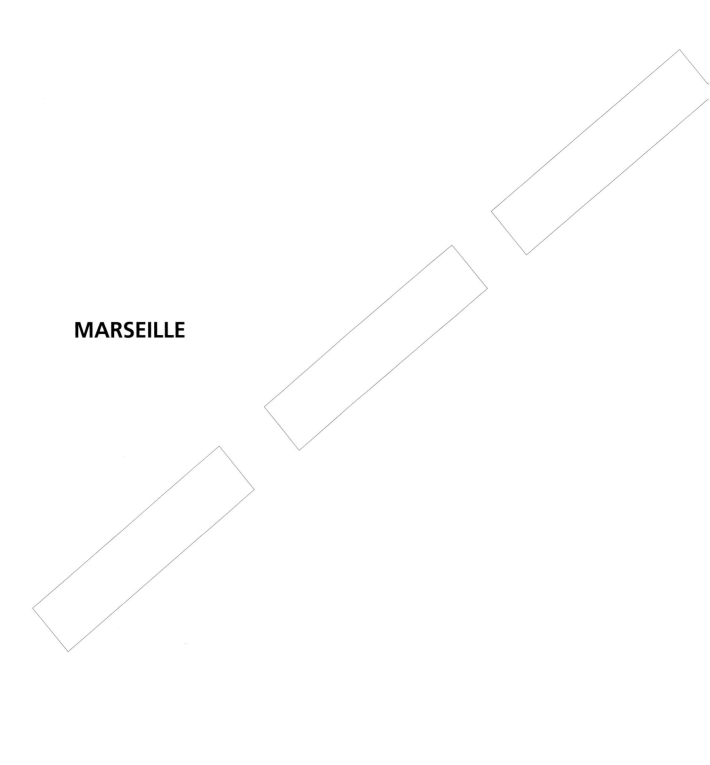

MARSEILLE

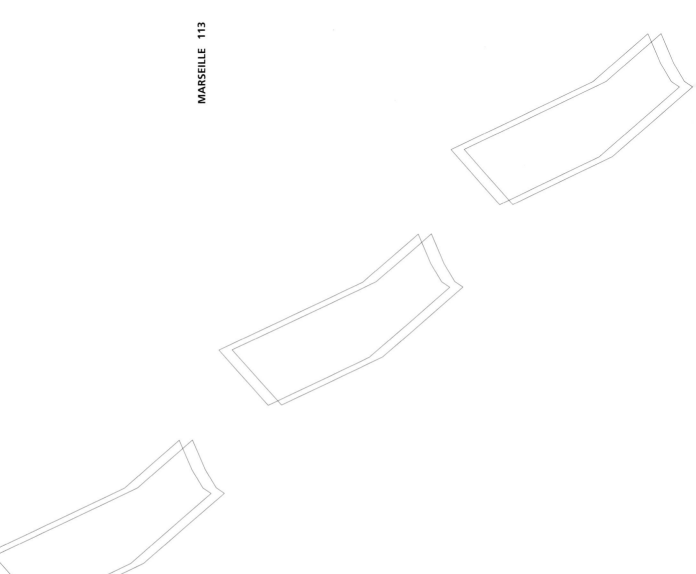

One of the earliest multiethnic cities, gateway to France or to the Orient, depending on where you happen to be standing. The first North African city in Europe. The well-known Unknown, a blank spot on the map even for the well-travelled. Red tiled floors. Apricot walls. Blue door frames. Black and white tensions.

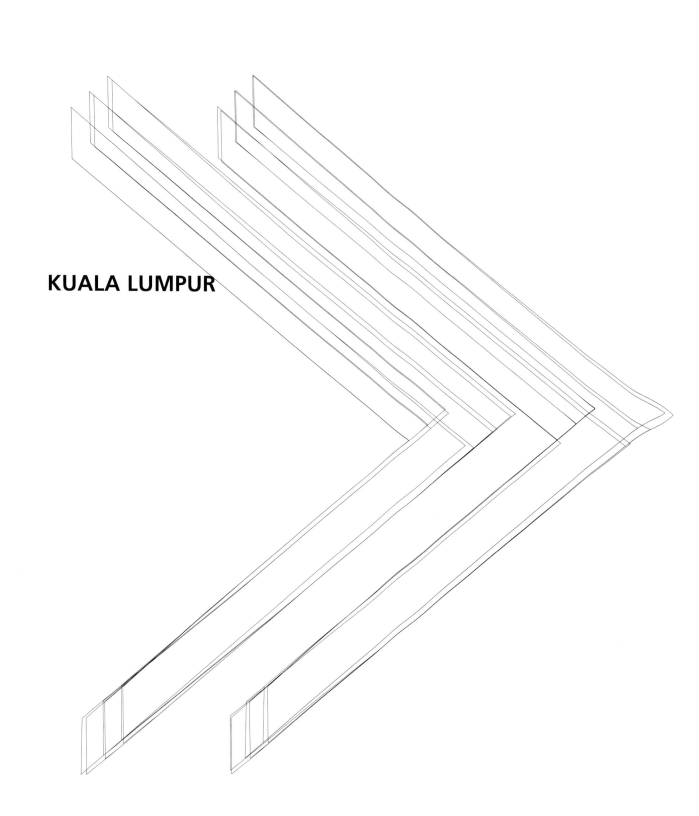

KUALA LUMPUR

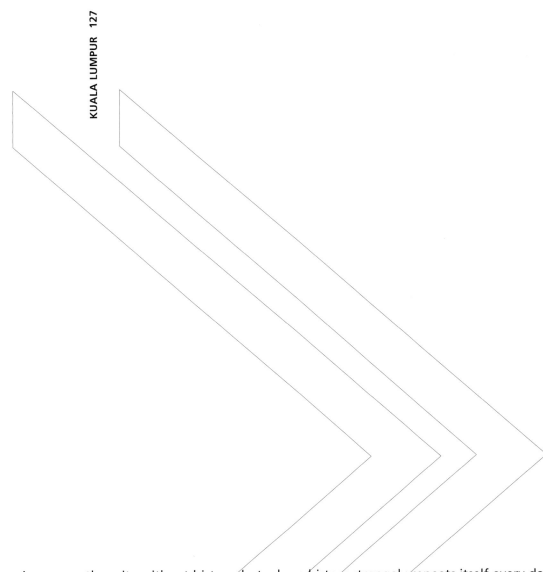

Kuala Lumpur is apparently a city without history, but where history strangely repeats itself every day. The conquest of the jungle through sheer optimism, the triumph of hope over doubt and of the daring over the meek are characteristics of this tropical boom town, now developing into a hitherto unknown form of post-metropolis.

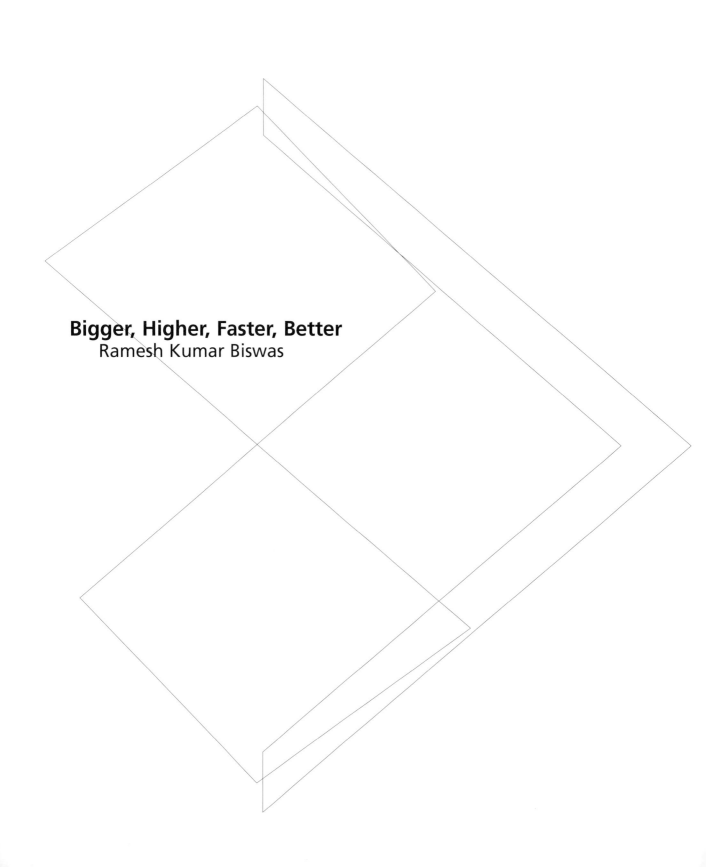

Bigger, Higher, Faster, Better
Ramesh Kumar Biswas

KUALA LUMPUR

A city can be like an individual, who, even as an adult, cannot entirely give up habits or patterns of behaviour familiar from his childhood. Kuala Lumpur is such a city, where events and people repeat their pasts in unexpected ways. Many seemingly inexplicable phenomena are easier to understand when viewed as variations of events that have taken place, or personalities that have appeared on the stage sometime during its densely packed history. This is surprisingly often the case for a place that actually believes it has no past, only a future.

There are two ways to look at urban history: one records people, events and places of value for their own sake; it calls for history to be cared for because "a city without old buildings is like a man without memory". The other sees history primarily as a tool to help us understand the present and the future, not a brake. Both these approaches may well be found in one and the same person (depending on where this person happens to be); which person may be against the indiscriminate destruction of the built heritage and the evolved structure of the city while in Malaysia; but which person, while in Europe, may fight against a conservationist mentality that prevents the expression of contemporary art and architecture. This is why the following account is not chronological. It switches back and forth between the founding era and the present, looking at the patterns of growth and conduct specific to this city; it is to be seen allegorically, not literally.

The peninsula of Malaya, the legendary "Golden Khersonese", is a perpetual crossroads and meeting place for adventurers, soldiers of fortune, mad geniuses and romantics. It was home to the earliest *homo sapiens* in Asia. But let us leave aside for the moment those who were hanging around here 40 000 years ago in settlements in the Stone Age, and who didn't bother even then to clear up their rubbish, later considered archaeological remains. The peninsula saw the development of numerous towns around 2000 years ago, arising from trade with India, Arabia, Indonesia and China. In the 7th and 8th centuries CE, these were powerful sea-going and trading city-states under the influence of the Sumatran Buddhist kingdom of Sri Vijaya, later they were governed from Hindu Java, with constant interference from Thailand.

Islam came in very early from Arabia – Marco Polo, on a Frequent Sailor programme in the 13th century, notes seeing Islamic communities. The coastal town of Melaka (Malacca) gradually became the most important city in South East Asia in mid-second millennium CE, showing an unexpectedly long urban tradition in an area commonly associated only with the 'jungle'. During all this time, merchants from North Asia, India and Arabia; tin miners from China and Ceylon; planters, missionaries and soldiers from Portugal, Holland and Britain brought

A City In Search Of A Continent
Jean-Claude Guillebaud

ISTANBUL

Extraordinary things are happening in Istanbul – a strange perturbance, an almost indefinable excitement; a certain confusion different from that in any other city. Is it a kind of exhuberance, the thrill of the exotic? It is not as simple as that; the feeling is much stronger. Just wander between the big bazaar and the docks, ascend the slopes of Pera or Galata that dip down to a sea "beset with cities of various colouring," or walk along the shade of the dilapidated Byzantine city wall and later take a taxi through the pulsating night life of the chic Bebek or Rumeli districts. One can sense that grand inspiration, a unique atmosphere and energy that has always distinguished this city. How can this metropolitan climate be best described? Is it the Levantine temperament or is it the vigour of this highly oriental city? Could it be the "unique humanity" that Flaubert reported? Is it the reminiscences of a decorative orientalismus lotis? Some are convinced that it is. But what makes Istanbul so exceptional? After all, the bazaars in Cairo, Jerusalem or Canaa can boast of just as much atmosphere, and the Omajjaden Mosque in Damascus is at least as enchanting as the Topkapi Serail or the Hagia Sophia. Is its breathtaking and unique geographical location between the Bosporus and the Golden Horn, that mythical link between Asia and Europe, the cross-roads of world trade that makes it so special? Possibly…

Chateaubriande believed this. "Constantinople", he tells his readers, "is the most beautiful place in the whole Universe". He exaggerated of course, perhaps because he had not seen enough of the universe. Did he ever visit the cradle of the Orient, approaching it from the African coast along the strait of Bab-El-Mandeb? Could he have been aware of how Asia presents itself so ceremoniously in Hong Kong's harbour? If Istanbul's splendour lay merely in its panoramic location, one could find several places in "the Universe" to equal it. What is it then? Some still claim that it is the uncanny concentration of races, customs, languages and traditions that lend Istanbul an incomparable cosmopolitan charm. Gérard de Neval was astonished at how "several nations could live here side-by-side without hating each other all too much." A beautiful notion, though basically conventional and even superficial when compared to melting pots like New York, Odessa or Shanghai… An even more specific and distinctive charm characterises Istanbul.

Where then does it come from? Why is it so undefinable? Both decisive factors in question here are related to atmosphere: to an enormous force added to a historic memory that goes so far back and is so persistent that one can barely gauge it. We know well how explosive the fusion of diverse molecules can be. And this is particularly true of Istanbul. For centuries now a project has been rumbling, growing and multiplying on the site of this city. This extraordinary capital has been in search of an empire worthy of it – a quality that has not been a secret to the city's observers ever since its incipience. For over a millennium, the Chinese have called Constantinople the "city of cities", and even in medieval times one spoke of no other place when conjuring the image of a perfect city. In fact the very name Istanbul appears to originate from the Byzantine expression "to The City" Dreaming of a socialist utopia at the beginning of the century, Charles Fourier, as Ghislain de Busbeck, felt that Istanbul would one day become "the capital of the world." It dominated the widespread Ottoman Empire. History has predicted an exceptional fate for this city on the sea, with luxuriant hills dipping down ever so magnificently to the shores of the Bosporus. It seems as though the site of the city has been imbued with an unfettered spirit from the very time of its origin.

Is it not true that its exceptional destiny now belongs to the past? Just speaking to the inhabitants of Istanbul, allowing them to speak of the past, urging them to paint a picture of the future would reveal that a continental nostalgia slumbers behind the facade of the Golden Horn. As the memory of a fabulous metropolis, the "mother of all cities" could turn their vision outwards once again and awaken the desire to push out the limits of the horizon. Such a vision could enrich one's experience of Istanbul and make it all the more exciting.

One should, however, begin one's experience of the city by contemplating and touching the remnants of the gigantic Byzantine city wall. Stretching all the way from the Marmara Sea to the Golden Horn, it did after all protect the city for several centuries. In order to comprehend Istanbul one has to begin with the historical question: What exactly did Constantinople symbolise a thousand years ago? What did it signify to Charlemagne's or Gottfried von Bouillon's contemporaries?

The capital of the East Roman Empire (Nea Roma, 'New Rome') and of Constantine, the man who lent the city its name, was more than just a symbol of Christianity. Enclosed within the protecting walls lay a geometric centre of civilisation. While the darkness of barbaric invasions and degeneration had spread over the West, while the pure brutality of the Dark Ages had befallen Europe, Constantinople embodied progressiveness. It was a magical city whose urban grandeur was one or even two centuries ahead of the rest of the world. It contained an unparalleled wealth of knowledge and riches that were not to be found elsewhere. The chronicles of the early crusades present a keen picture of how exceptionally advanced the city was; innumerable palaces and statues, marble paved squares, wide streets flanked with trees, an arena with 30 000 seats, the Hagia Sophia, whose dome swelled 51 metres high. What the crusaders from a primitive Europe beheld in the year 1096 was not just an enormous city but a wholly new planet for them. Constantinople must have seemed as unreal, enigmatic and "futuristic" to the European as today's Manhattan would to a soldier from Napoleon's army. This awe remained unabated for nine centuries, and I am not sure whether we will ever overcome it.

Even much later, the glory of the city now called Istanbul remained undiminished and comparable to that of an unforgettable Constantinople. With the Ottoman conquest and the collapse of Byzantine, one empire was replaced by another in the city on the Bosphorus. Though religion and language changed, the laws that were laid at its birth still remain. Despite the change of name and nationality, the "High Portal" mysteriously retained the spirit of the site. Byzantium, Constantinople, Istanbul – how is one to resist the magical charm that every successive incarnation of the same urban energy radiates?

Observe the introspective stance of visitors looking at the boundless extent of the Ottoman Empire depicted in the mural map in Topkapi Museum. Faced with this awesome imperial topography, the visitor is invariably overawed and impressed. One is hit by the knowledge that this was once the seat of the greatest empire ever, extending from Persia to the gates of Vienna and from Tangiers to the Upper Nile. And it withstood the trials of almost half a millennium. "So this was Istanbul, the city of the Khedive and the janissaris, the central nervous system of an immeasurable power", is what the gestures of the visitors seemed to convey.

The amicable Orientalism, with a colonial touch, that pervaded travel literature at the end of the nineteenth century, is older than one thinks. Seen in a historical context, writers had only caught a brief glimpse of the city. Mark Twain and Reuter were among those who came here at that time. It was a moment in which Istanbul had regressed to the charms of a commonplace oriental metropolis: the usual picturesque concoction of the archaic and the enchanting, of turbaned bureaucrats, hookah smokers, whirling dervishes and belly dancers. We still tend to see the city with the eyes of those obsessed with exoticism. But Istanbul has long since rid itself of the kitsch of oriental folklore. It would be wrong to assume that, with the fall of the Ottoman Empire, Istanbul forfeited its legacy of a preordained, exceptional spirit it had inherited from Byzantium and Constantinople. Seen in a historical context, a metropolis like Istanbul (Rome or Athens had long passed their zenith of glory) expresses its energy in a different way. I believe that the remarkable rise of Kemalism that began in the 20s followed Istanbul's grand objectives.

What was the essence of Kemal Attaturk's political credo? It was an accelerated metamorphosis, a daring yet brutal venture. In attempting to turn the young republic into a modern and progressive country within the span of less than a generation, Mustafa Kemal catapulted the Turks and Istanbul into an unparalleled adventure. He secularised the state, introduced the Latin script, emancipated the women and demanded a new way of life. No other ruler seeking to modernise his country had ever dared take such strides in such a short time.

For Istanbul, this drastic swerve towards modernity was accompanied by a concrete geographical shift. The city, set on both banks of the Bosporus, one half Oriental and the other European, now tilted more to the West in keeping with the country's will to unite with Europe. Istanbul had trams. Connecting passageways were built through the city. The film industry was founded and even an underground railway was planned. And the men had to shave off their beards.

How could one describe the city without mentioning Kemalism? Kemal's traces are ubiquitous and his success omnipresent. Istanbul as a modern city comprises more than Teheran, Cairo or Baghdad do. Its modernity is not limited to architecture, to technology or to the demonstration of a creed. It manifests itself in the way children are brought up, in the culture as well as in the activities of the state. Modernism is evident in the history of every family in Istanbul. As time passed, they all absorbed it. While dining in a restaurant in the University area or when invited to a meal in the open, or while seated on the terraces along the banks of the Bosphorus one sees people – professors, students and businesspeople of either sex – and they are no different from their counterparts in Paris, London or Hamburg. "The very basis of the Turkish republic is the emancipation of women. Contrary to all Western expectations, it is our country's greatest social achievement in this century", says the engineer and theatre director Yilmaz Onay.

Seven decades of Kemalism, three generations and the inhabitants of the city have produced today's Istanbul, which is now under pressure from 'Asian', muslim, rural, anti-international groups. A completely new Istanbul is emerging, where nine-tenths of the present inhabitants were not born in the city.

The present day megalopolis dominates historical Istanbul – Dogan Kuban, urban historian, sees it as the anti-Istanbul. The area covered by today's conglomeration is about twenty times larger than the historical city. Enclosing the familiar Istanbul, this megalopolis is *terra incognita* and no one, not even the city administration or the central government, has reliable knowledge of it. Single aspects of its existence can perhaps be studied or described, but its true being remains a puzzle. It certainly is no formal city. The social and physical structure of the city has changed so radically that a qualitative rift now divides the Istanbul of the Fifties, or that of the Sixties from the Istanbul of the present. Plans can not steer its development; they no longer define the future but solely record already concluded developments.

As a resident of the city, Yilmaz Onay experiences the situation so: "You can never understand Istanbul without knowledge of its historical roots, of its struggles of cultural interaction, or of its historical conflicts. What I try to sense from the past or the present of a city is the everyday life of its citizens, their joys and their fears. That is the only way I can learn to love its buildings, streets and squares. For instance, what created a lasting impression on me while visiting the excavations in Ephesos was an antique pictogram: a stone with a circle and a line, indicating the way to a brothel in the city. Questions related to city development and equality have haunted me every since I became interested in the anthropology of cities, which actually began when I started studying the history of the Amazons in Anatolya.

Old or new, I have always loved places with their own distinct atmosphere and therefore also my city, the world city that is Istanbul. When you see old photographs of Istanbul, you will surely discern the differences between the city as it was then and it is now. Today, some are trying to turn Istanbul into a city coloured by fundamentalism. Contrary to the widespread opinion, this is not due to the flood of immigrants from Anatolya's small towns. It is not so much the immigrants from the rural parts of the country, who usually only try to adapt themselves to the city, but the fundamentalists charged with political fervour who are trying to hold the city to siege, even subjugate it.

This drive for power finds expression in the increasing violence in Istanbul. They say that Istanbul is transformed every four to five years, but the changes during the last five years are threatening to become historical turning points. Ever-increasing segments of the city's society are now turning into obdurate totalitarian and fundamentalist structures."

So who is on top? Who makes the music? Who are the Istanbulians? Stephan Yerasimos, urban historian, says, "If the authorities would lock up people in their homes in Istanbul on a Sunday and then count them, would we know exactly how many people live in the city? Certainly not! For the numbers we expect are supposed to gauge the uncountable. No such number exists. What we expect of these numbers, provided us by statistical institutions can, at best, convince us of the fact that a continually elusive reality is impossible to comprehend. A few months after it was held, the October 1995 census revealed the population of Istanbul and its environs to be seven million. Available data would lead to the conclusion that the population would actually be ten million in 1997. The man on the street, the taxi driver, the housewife and the public servant would be all outraged if you mentioned the official numbers. They consider it to be an impertinence to imply that the sea of humanity that they struggle against everyday numbers "only" ten million! According to unofficial accounts, the real number is more like twelve or even fifteen million, in reality it is perhaps even higher. At any rate, this is what the chaos on the street seems to suggest.

Even the 1997 census is assumed to be fantastical. One tells each other anecdotes of houses, settlements, of entire districts in Istanbul where no census authority has ever set foot. Officials are accused of being utterly incompetent and Machiavellian, but finally one falls backs into a fatalistic attidude as the only way to come to terms with all the excess. This refusal to accept reality, a reality that can only be fragmentary and imprecise, is by definition the only way out. It is, therefore, also a palpable expression of the physical and mental incapacity to grasp Istanbul's growing agglomeration. Whether immigration is affecting Istanbul negatively or positively is an irrelevant question. The process will nevertheless continue at the same pace and rhythm for the next quarter of a century. The city, whose population has already multiplied itself ten times in 50 years, will by then have doubled itself and reached the 20 million mark. The introduction of radical measures to stall immigration, with the enforcement of visas or even the threat of expulsion is just a figment of Istanbulian fantasy.

Faced with dramatic environmental destruction, the citizens of Istanbul feel furiously helpless. Not only is their everyday life onerous but even their history is being destroyed beyond recognition with every passing day, so they tend to call for radical solutions. Enraged, they demand strong and efficient urban law and order to give the city new meaning. They call for a strong state to enforce harsh laws to tame a reality one never even attempted to become acquainted with before. This is perhaps the most dangerous vision of the future in Istanbul".

Even in 1147, the traveller Odon de Deuil considered it a city "disproportionate in all ways". Only 30% of the residents enjoy social services, education, employment rights and pensions as guaranteed by law. An army commander has an income of €1170, a schoolteacher only €420, the rest who eke their living selling on the street, even less. 20% of these uncounted millions are unemployed. A glance at the new street map – a volume containing over 300 segments of the city – shows an imposing picture of what is understood as urban development in metropolitan Istanbul. The areas marked green denote the forested hinterland, whereas the light yellow ones are unidentifiable, illegal *gecekondu* settlements, where rural migrants settle. Streets that have been drawn in greater detail show how the simple and still rural structure of huts and houses has been replaced by multi-storeyed concrete structures along a suburban pattern. The migrants are from East and Central Anatolya. Immediately on arrival they pitch a tent or a group of tents next to the parked cars. Here we encounter the *gecekondu* pioneers again, whose houses will turn to stone the moment a worthless entry in the land register allows building on communal land. Urban planners Eva Maria Froschauer and Volker Martin describe this phenomenon in a study:

"Of course, these settlements are all as illegal as the multi-storeyed houses that have rapidly sprouted all over the region. This land, too, on which the immigrants set up their first shelters, defies all regulatory measures. Since Islamic Law sees it as asylum, this 'overnight' housing is protected from being demolished. Clever developers are now even building completely illegal high-rise buildings or entire developments only at night, without building permission.

Gradual legalisation of *gecekondu* housing was followed by overbuilding and remodelling, so much so that the settlements began to liken suburban towns. Such heterogeneous and anarchist architecture, the result of unrestricted development without setback regulations or vertical zoning laws (Istanbul's town development allows only four floors), gradually became legalised. Speculation hiked property prices and led to a further concen-

tration of buildings on an "urban" model. It is only now that infrastructure and services are being introduced. The urban structure required by law in the settlement area, such as channelling traffic by widening streets as well as an 'Islamisation' of the squares has necessitated continual rebuilding, which has completely obliterated the thirty-year long history of these districts. All forms of land encroachment appear here simultaneously. Losing no time, the 'real estate mafia' swooped in and planted numerous multi-storeyed houses amongst the improvised preliminary 'shelters'. These properties are built with few and simple materials, immediately looking older than they actually are.

Though always illegal, it is no longer the rapid upgrading of the *gecekondus* that marks an unprecedented development but the newer illegal buildings and wild construction dominate even close to the city centre. The real reason is rather a wild growth of unauthorised construction, unrestricted in style or size. Only the up-market areas near the centre are subjected to basic norms of land allotment, blocks and public space. Whether privately financed, speculative, or organised by co-operatives, all housing projects in Istanbul are faced with the misuse of power by local officials who simply ignore all land use plans. Local interests which do not take a complete view of the city, bribes and deals where "one hand washes the other", as well as blackmail, govern business transactions. Building permits are quickly and easily obtained with "improvement plans" for land that was so far spared from illegal development. Although extensive regulatory laws are passed from time to time, the 1995 research report – a tangle of statistics with confusing and colourful drawings – cannot conceal a tendency to dress up the facts.

Renewal, even though it happened without a trace of planning, did somehow convert this informal settlement around the core into a kind of real 'city' by improving public infrastructure. Building speculation does create the impression for the common man that "at least something is happening". Besides it stimulates the 'informal' economy and creates employment, and is a factor not to be ignored. Near the intellectual and religious centres – the mosques – squares and bazaars have emerged, urbanising the settlements if only at a basic level. Even if only sheep are shepherded here and a twisted hydrant possibly bears witness to a functioning water supply, this still marks a gradual progress from the rural to the urban. Where absolutely nothing is planned any more, where investment just happens to find its plot, where city space is born of nothing but audacious speculation, the rape of land and soil seems to be the rule. To make matters worse, yet another amnesty law was passed in favour of these 'overnight constructions' during the 1999 elections, and such laws are expected for every election to come.

There seems to be no room for new and optimistic ideas. Both Istanbul's town planners, Sinan Bölek and Seben Yüzer comment on the 1995 master plan with the usual lack of vision and make the obvious but empty statement: "Without cooperation between state and local officials, the city will be faced with a disaster – with no way out."

In these out-of-control settlements there are bars, nightclubs, mosques, Dervish clubs, Marxist cells, rural communities, workers' organisations. Has the city become entirely easternised as it was once forcefully westernised? Not in the least! Istanbul's history is alive with contradictions. Turkish migrant workers in the West and their offspring are introducing Western values, while on the Eastern front, the recent past presents the most astonishing changes of all. Just watch a plane land at the international airport. Who is it that gets off the plane, night or day? Some tourists from the West, of course.

But look around the airport more attentively. The majority of passengers does not consist of tourists. An unending stream of other visitors pours out: Turkmens, Kirgise, Uzbeks and Tazaks, to mention just a few nationalities. Resolute men and women, often clad in humble, even picturesque attire from distant lands, lug enormous shopping bags, huge suitcases and enormous sacks. With their luggage bursting at the seams, they talk loudly and seem to be in a frightful hurry. This is obviously not their first visit to Istanbul. Were you to follow them you would end up in the main bazaar, where they almost immediately start haggling, and then they stuff their bags with stupendous quantities of wares. Then they go away. But they come back. And go away again.

Who are all these people? What does all the bustle mean? Everybody knows that citizens from the Central Asian republics of the former USSR have now found their way back to Istanbul after the dissolution of the Soviet empire. The city is oriental and so are they; they are

Muslims, and they too speak a Turkish tongue. One is tempted to believe that their coming to Istanbul is most natural, that they are attracted by the surplus of goods, which stands in stark contrast to the scarcity in Tashkent or whichever city they come from. They come to Istanbul with the sole purpose of shopping and trading. What's so surprising about that? Doesn't Istanbul also attract people from the Baltic, from cities like Wilna or Talinn for the very same reason?

For Muslims from the former USSR, this continuation of exchange with Istanbul is much more than mere trade. The collapse of the Soviet Union reverted the Central Asian Muslim republics to their age-old customs that had a greater affinity to Istanbul than to Moscow. The expanding trade, the regularly sold-out flights – all point at historical bonds. These ties that are rapidly forming again were once so versatile diverse and, in reality, unlimited. In the old city one comes across groups of men with burnt faces and rustic manners, wearing turbans and ballooned trousers. For these people, Istanbul is once again the "big city".

The city, on the other hand, begins to vibrate again through this natural process of exchange. North and West open out once again into an enormous cultural area comprising a large number of impoverished and unstable states, all in search of a metropolis – and an identity.

A simple facial expression, a look, can suggest an answer. Just continue your stroll about the streets. You would also encounter young, veiled women in the bazaar, in the University campus, just everywhere. Stacks of books, video cassettes, compact discs and posters in praise of Islam fill the shops. There is an unconcealed, yet silent nostalgia for the Ottoman Empire. Pop singers praise Allah or curse Attaturk, the father of modern Istanbul, with full-throated gusto.

How is this possible in the capital of Kemalism? Islamic rituals in the heart of secular and modern Istanbul? They are indeed possible. What is acted out on the streets, parks and quays is indicative of the ongoing alchemic processes in the secret depths of the city. In spite of the backdrop of this most incredible panorama, the visitor is left with an uncanny feeling that Istanbul's soul has imperceptibly escaped to the other side of the Bosporus. It seems as though the city, having turned its back to Europe, were now looking toward Central Asia, toward the stony planes of Anatolya and the minarets of Konya from which the *muezzin* summon the faithful to prayer.

SOWETO

Urban space is political, nowhere more blatantly so than in Soweto, vast incarceration camp and hotbed of resistance. One cannot expect to find beauty or comfort in cities as one did in the past. Soweto is a household word, a prototype, a symbol of an increasing number of similar places elsewhere, the 'suburb' or 'slum' that takes over and co-determines the main city, political arena for the poor, the dispossesed. Yet it has its own unique, powerful identity, valiantly turning its tragic past into strength for survival today.

The Dis-Location
Henning Rasmuss

SOWETO

Until a few years ago, an outsider whose knowledge of South Africa arose solely from the consumption of international media may have been forgiven for thinking of Johannesburg as a suburb of Soweto, which is where the real action is. Yes, Johannesburg is near Soweto. It's right over there, behind the mine dumps. Yes, over there, where you can see the bright lights.

But Soweto itself is no longer simply what it is, it is a symbol. Its name encapsulates many Sowetos all over the world, it embodies so many other places, systems and ideas. Soweto is an idea of an environment, a model. Though Soweto is typical of many such places, it is also its own place. Only one of many townships near Johannesburg, it has its own story.

If you speak of the urban landscape of Johannesburg, you have to speak of its shadow cities, of those other places just visible on the horizon, behind the mine dumps. In the foreground is Johannesburg, e-Goli, Place of Gold, born of opportunity and greed, a grown-up gold rush frontier town, the metropolis of the Southern hemisphere – once 'the principal white city in Africa', now the arena of a Euro-African urban cultural synthesis. But behind Johannesburg there lurks the other city, the city more notorious, more violent, more populated, more problematic, more short-lived and more self-confident: Soweto.

Soweto seems to many to have been born in June 1976, when it exploded into the world's conscience through the violence of the student demonstrations. The events of those weeks focused world attention on South Africa and the struggle against apartheid, and Soweto became synonymous with resistance to the system that shaped it and perfected its form.

Apartheid (Afrikaans for separate-ness) as a system of spatial order was all about control over people and material in space. Apartheid: an enforced, statutory way of delineating territories, placing bodies, directing economics, channeling production, restricting contact, dividing groups, policing people and emphasising ethnicity. Even the town's name conjures no Zulu rhythms but originates from this official spatial ordering system, simultaneously evil and banal: SoWeTo – South Western Township. At the height of the apartheid oppression in the eighties, a ministry was established that dealt with policing, known as the Ministry of Law and Order. At an abstract level, apartheid was a type of spatial practice, in essence, 'Raumordnung' (spatial order). Part of the perverse parlance of the apartheid regime was that the ministry for enforcing state repression carried a name with strong planning connotations. And one of its primary devices was control over the urban black population through the layout and design of the townships.

It is easy to equate the townships of South Africa with the system of apartheid. However, Johannesburg's urban layout has a somewhat longer history. As a fully developed and institutionalised system, apartheid came into existence only after the National Party came to power in 1948. The spatial practice of townships had by then been long established, indeed, apartheid merely formalised and perfected a pre-existing spatial construct entrenched since the 19th century. Forcible removals of the black population started in 1906. The Urban Areas Act of 1923/24 formalized this trend. A systematic evacuation of black people to subsidized housing south of the city began, to the area that became known in the 60s as Soweto. So in order to understand Soweto, we need to look further back to the forces that shaped Johannesburg as a whole, and then at its form.

South Africa is basically a non-urban country, as anyone who has traversed it will testify. 'City' is the exception in the landscape. But where 'city' occurs in this land, it impacts dramatically on the order of life. Johannesburg, of desperate hope and violent exploitation, was invented in a mad rush of industrial activity after 1886. It would be too easy to dismiss it, as many do, as characterless and uncultivated. It has always devoured people, and has always held a fascination for those viewing it from a distance. The story of the growth of Johannesburg is also the story of urbanisation in South Africa. And Soweto is a part of that chain of events. From the very beginning the mines relied on cheap labour, since the gold deposits were not concentrated. By 1897, half of the population of Johannesburg was made up of blacks who had come to the city directly from the land. The labourers were never treated as full residents of the city and were always relegated to 'temporary' settlements on the city fringes. Parts of Soweto, such as Moroka Township, started out as shack settlements with such names as 'Amasaka', meaning 'sack shelter' Soweto has always struggled to become a 'real' city, struggled against

a never-ending stream of migrants, against impermanence and against attempts to deny its very existence.

Urbanisation is, of course, not unique to South Africa. But the structure of South African society, long before apartheid, certainly added its own impetus to the development of cities like Johannesburg. The 1913 'Natives Land Act' effectively deprived blacks of land ownership, giving 87% of the land over to white ownership. The result was impoverishment of the rural communities, a constant stream of migrant labour into the cities, and a growing class of urban poor who lived on the fringes of society. Rural families participated in the urban economy by selling the labour of one or more family members to the mines or the expanding factories.

Uncontrolled urbanisation had become common by the outbreak of World War Two, and the institutionalisation of apartheid in 1948 was in part a (racist) response to the previous failure of the State to develop and implement a coherent urbanisation policy. There never was security of tenure, and long before the forced removals of apartheid, health legislation was used to control the growth of 'non-white' urban areas. In 1904, the so-called 'coolie' and 'kaffir' locations were burnt to the ground after an outbreak of bubonic plague. The area was replanned and renamed as 'Newtown', and its residents were relocated to the Klipspruit Location. This, the first project of 'urban renewal' in Johannesburg barely 18 years after its birth set the pattern for all subsequent attempts at controlling the urban black population, moving it further and further away from the city centre.

By 1923, the 'Natives (Urban Areas) Act' formalised what was to become known as the practice of 'influx control'. It was based on the strategy of total residential segregation of the 'races', and the absence of security of tenure for blacks. "The Native should only be allowed to enter the urban areas, which are essentially the white man's creation, insofar as he is required to minister to the needs of the white man and should depart therefrom when he ceases so to minister" – this from the report by the government commission appointed to investigate urbanisation in 1922. There is a particular strangeness to the way that South African urbanisation has occurred: while the process itself may be universal, the management of it in these urban areas has its own peculiar logic and results in its own extraordinary political geography.

"'Home' is an appropriated place; it does not exist objectively…The notion of 'home' is a fiction we create out of a need to belong. Home is a place most people have never been to. Home serves a function similar to zero in mathematics. It provides us with a beginning or a basis from which to evaluate other spaces…" says the Johannesburg photographer Santu Mofokeng. The 'Group Areas Act' of 1950 formalised segregation even further and formed the cornerstone of the 'Homeland' system. Under the notorious 'Pass Laws', permits regulated the access, movement and location of each and every black citizen of the country. The 'homelands' acted as labour reserves and as decentralised industrial nodes, in an attempt at slowing the influx of blacks into the urban areas. The system set up to control the urban black population bore in it the contradictions which led to the ultimate demise of apartheid. The logic of the consumer society was denied to these disenfranchised urban dwellers who enjoyed only temporary status in their place of residence, but who were expected to show allegiance to an abstract, ethnically-defined 'homeland' in the rural areas. The system of 'labour bureaux' in the homelands was perhaps the most transparent part of a system that perpetuated the accumulation of capital based on cheap labour in the cities, with the 'excess population' being shunted to the peripheries.

The planning of townships, then, was undertaken in conjunction with the requirements of industry. The insecurity of the township residents, coupled with the attempts at a peculiar form of central government planning and management, prevented any coherent and structured urban planning for places like Soweto. The more the miners worked, the more they contributed to the transformation of the veld into a job-creating, income-generating city. Johannesburg generated its wealth from the township residents during the day, relegating them to the outlying 'dormitory cities' at night, where they were forbidden to run businesses. The status of 'dormitory city' bestowed on Soweto led to an artificial imbalance in the normal distribution of urban functions and activities. The 'social engineering' of the townships before and during the years of apartheid had its economic consequences: lacking its own businesses, the city of Soweto had no tax base from which to generate income. As a purely residential settlement, commercial functions in the sprawl of houses were restricted to the bare minimum. To this day, Johannesburg city is the shopping centre for Soweto's residents. Soweto had no legal industries, commercial or service infrastructure of its own, and the wealth generated by its workers was predominantly diverted to the betterment of 'white' urban areas. The 'Separate Amenities Act' ensured the provision of separate services for different ethnic groups, from schools to clinics to libraries to recreation facilities, although the distribution clearly favoured the 'white' group areas. This inevitably led to resentment and to the increasing politicisation of the issue of official service provision.

As a result of its controlled dormitory city status, Soweto could never develop into a 'normal' city as may have happened in a slum anywhere else in the world. Added to the imbalance of income and concentration of the poor in Soweto was the high cost of transport in relation to wages. The apartheid urban system is perhaps the most wasteful ever devised. Putting distances between people was a fundamental principle as opposed to the practical 'city of short distances' that existed elsewhere and that has recently reemerged as a concept of desirable planning. The ideological State separated communities to the maximum degree, doubled on every category of public service provision for every single ethnic or 'racial' group, and then proceeded to subsidise the resulting wasteful system from State funds. Transport provision became one of the major structuring factors of the urban landscape, and Soweto's residents have always been part of a daily army of millions of commuters who have to cross the artificial functional and racial boundaries of South Africa's cities.

One could say that at an abstract level, the townships were culturally and socially 'invisible'. So complete was the segregation that even today, you will find few Johannesburgers who have ever been to Soweto. The two groups were "tourists in each other's worlds", as Lindsay Bremner, professor at Witwatersrand University and former chair of the Housing, Urbanization and Environmental Management Committees in Jo'burg Metropolitan Council after the change of regime, puts it. She states that the divisions between people have been blurred since 1994 not so much through the efficacies of a moral urban administration but rather through new, less normative logics – those of necessity, speculation and crime. The culture of the townships is only now beginning to be revealed and recorded. The social engineering project of South African society has probably nowhere been more successful than in this respect. While black residents of Soweto worked in Johannesburg during the day and were at least able to observe 'white' life, the white residents of Johannesburg could not be more ignorant about Soweto than if a physical wall had been erected between the two places. Soweto is 'known' through grainy black-and-white images of houses huddled under a hazy sky, of demonstrating school students, of inscrutable violence, murder, destitution - seldom a positive image. The material reality and the daily human experience of township life is hidden behind a transparent screen – a screen constructed by ideology and fear, by difference and the inability to deal with 'otherness'.

The urban 'Native Housing Policy' was a cornerstone of the apartheid project. While it would be easy to dismiss this policy as a set of wild, irrational punitive measures carried out by an insane authoritarian state, this is too simple an interpretation of the actions of an almost perfectly organized, if morally suspect, system of government. Instead, the housing programme formed part of a deliberate, carefully constructed framework of domination enacted through political and technical strategies. Soweto served as an arena for the enactment of ideology in the form of bricks and mortar. The urban framework of apartheid was already entrenched in the spatial layout of Johannesburg. The technical framework was created through the co-option of professionals, including architects, in a 'scientific' research programme aimed at optimising the production of living space within the existing ideological construct.

If we were to read the urban landscape of Soweto through the discourse of Michel Foucault, we could uncover something of the power/form relationships that guided the management of black urban areas. Whilst it is too simplistic to equate Foucault's carceral city of disciplinary institutions with places like Soweto, the barrack-like order of houses and the constant, prison-like policing of the township populations by agencies of the State were clearly physical manifestations of exclusive urban political power and domination. The problem of housing the growing urban black population has been debated and addressed since the late 1930's. The social agenda of European modernism such as the La Sarraz Declaration of 1928, which focused on the social implications of architectural practice and stressed the construction of housing over that of prestigious buildings, provided the intellectual background. However, local planners were already critical of le Corbusier's 'City of Tomorrow' and the Ville Radieuse in 1941, politically suspect due to their basis in environmental determinism.

The discourse then shifted towards generating a formal model for housing. Social validity was to be regained through 'science'. A belief in value-free architectural engagement at the technical level was sought through an 'accurate' analysis of existing context and 'practical' solutions for implementation. An ideal of non-idealistic practice was posited for the profession. Idealism in practice was relegated to a secondary position, to be pursued in times of 'lesser social stress'. The ideological trap in this line of argumentation led the profession to accept, as a 'given' restraint, pre-existing 'contextual' conditions such as racial segregation. It was this ability to remove the political dimension from the realm of professional action that allowed architects to be co-opted into supporting the ideology of the regime.

Another pre-existing condition was the basically anti-urban focus of modernist town planning, imported by European-trained town planners in local government after the Second World War. Soweto is a case study in the application of an anti-city ethos. In formal terms, the free-standing building in open space is seen as the basic building block of the urban system. The pavilion type on an open plot is seen as the basis of 'good' urban life. The approach to development promotes suburban rather than urban values. Coupled with the scientific method of deriving housing solutions is the arithmetic derivation of urban functions. Groups of individual units give rise to programs of standardised infrastructure, whereby X number of units gives rise to a primary school, Y number to a high school, and Z units substantiate the provision of a clinic. Activities are separated into monofunctional areas in order to reduce conflict between functions. Urban growth occurs through the addition of complete township units to the urban pattern, rather than through incremental growth. In practice, the modernist constructs of town planning fitted smoothly into the ideological programme of apartheid. Urban space functioned solely as a buffer between races and classes and allowed the pursuit of the ideal of separation.

The government euphemistically labelled apartheid as 'separate development'. The central building block for urban growth was the 'neighbourhood unit'. In Soweto in particular, these principles were subverted by the apartheid administration to the point where ethnic groups were accommodated in separate neighbourhood cells, with separate schools, community facilities, clinics – optimising the spatial and cultural separation between groups in the urban areas. If we take a look at Soweto today we can clearly see the ideology in the plan. Buffer strips of open land separate the ethnic areas within Soweto. The roads are neatly laid out in a police-friendly fashion. Visible in the plan, too, is the strident belief in the power of technology to transform the nature of society. Thus the road network, the pattern of engineering efficiency. The European bias in the spatial models is clearly visible. It is surely perverse to structure and scale a settlement around the motor car where the population is not, even today, individually mobile. The inward-focusing, convoluted road network supports the aim of spatial segregation and division according to racial and ethnic groups at the expense of environmental quality.

There is something strangely romantic about the drawings published at the time, which show the bucolic garden setting of a pavilion house amongst trees. Perhaps these are the closest reminders of the anti-urban ethos of the Garden City movement. There was never any question that the state would subsidise 'African' housing that was not 'economical'. This, against the background of the impermanent status of urban blacks, led to the increasing focus on the individual unit as the measure of production. The social element was in theory still part of the programme, but did not form part of the realisation. The proposed community centres, shopping facilities and parks were never developed. In their place, desolate left-over pieces of land separated one set of monotonous houses from another. Houses were constructed, but not communities. The spatial arrangement of free-standing houses placed in the middle of open 'gardens' did lend itself to control and policing in times of conflict and protest. In that sense, the Foucaultesque reading of Soweto's layout is not entirely misplaced.

These faceless, featureless, polluted, anti-social environments, devoid of any real social infrastructure, are monuments to apartheid. Soweto has been described by the architect and political activist Clive Chipkin as the 'City of Stress'. The social abnormalities that were part of the system, such as the single-sex hostels for migrant workers, injected enormous conflict into the lives of its population. Alienation, physical insecurity, hostility, depersonalisation and lack of identity were symptoms of social failure that characterised daily life. In retrospect, one can say that predominantly white architects and planners colluded in the creation of the physical form of Soweto. Their social and intellectual failure lay in the attempt to approach the provision of housing as an aesthetic and technical discourse, artificially separated from political and economic issues, though of course this is also familiar from other places and periods.

What will become of Soweto and what is it like now? What remains is a 150 square kilometre area which harbours anything between two and four million people. Most of the literature on Soweto stems from the time of oppression, when it was notorious as a hotbed of opposition. Most writings mythologise and caricaturise the city. It is a distorted image of reality, both in resistance and oppression. Experiencing it today is sobering - Soweto is an environmental failure. There is no point in denying that. It is also a city still plagued by the artificially constructed abnormalities of a finally expired regime.

South Africa has been liberated. Johannesburg has been liberated. Apartheid has been replaced by new systems of government at national and local level. But Soweto will be with us for a long time. The townships did not empty overnight, the homes of millions will continue to be just that: homes in which daily life continues. Urbanisation hurtles on, even more chaotic than before. The economic base of Soweto is still unbalanced. Housing policy is now a tool of development rather than oppression, however, the spatial model of the township still holds. The free-standing single-storey house is the type demanded by those who have been promised shelter by the democratically elected government. The land around will be overrun by thousands of small, free-standing houses, in practice no better than the apartheid patterns that have made up Soweto since the 1950's. The low-density urban sprawl continues, compounding the problems of the urban poor, stretching limited resources and necessitating ever-increasing commuting distances.

A new terror reigns the night. Horrifying killings, rapes and robberies are but only part of the picture. What is striking today is how 'normal' everything is. Beyond the old black-and-white photographs, here is life in full colour. Normal people, shopping at the local 'Spaza Shop' or getting an outrageous hair-do. Because of the lack of commercial infrastructure, individual entrepreneurs have opened up hundreds of shops in garages, houses, front and back rooms. Anything goes, from car washes to rickety taxi stands to hairdressers with fantastic illustrations to bread and milk corners to drinking holes to exhaust repair workshops. The territorial restrictions are ignored, the functional separation subverted. The street becomes inhabited.

Lindsay Bremner notes that today largely illicit ways of controlling, managing and using urban space challenge its rules: "Necessity has driven the urban poor to reinvent the city and so challenge the utopianism of modernist planning. People live in cracks, cook on the streets, bed down on the pavements; shops appear on street corners; warehouses shelter families; office blocks become factories; houses turn into shops; chickens, goats, mealies appear on inner city curbs; Taiwanese watches are displayed next to Nigerian bags, next to local tomatoes. The old oppositions between urban and rural, public and private, residential and business, black and white merge in indistinguishable new combinations; boundaries are porous; peoples merge; the city is vitally, colourfully grey. The normalization of this spontaneity, in the interests of good governance, is no longer possible – the scale of the intervention required and the management of its consequences lies beyond the scope of the democratic, neo-liberal state; and even if it were possible, it would bring to the surface hosts of networks upon whose invisibility the fragile economic survival of the city's poor depends".

Noticeable is the sense of community, the friendliness. People everywhere exchanging greetings, waving, hooting. The traffic is chaotic, somewhat different from Johannesburg. Tiny houses, stacked close together. In the quieter streets, meticulous care has been taken to domesticise a garden: trimmed hedges, a car tyre is cut in half to make a plant stand. A nice suburban setting for your NE 51/9 house. Along the busier roads, more shops crowding the front gardens, spilling onto the street. Everywhere, building activity. The existing building systems are often difficult to convert. An incredible inventiveness comes into play. How does one add on to such impossibly minimal houses? Often, the existing house disappears inside the shell of a new one that is built around it. The outer wall becomes an inner wall. One house swallows another, one political identity another. Space is reclaimed, the monotony is broken. New and different forms, materials, functions invade and replace the programmatic township scene.

"Are we evolving a split personality which may generate its own forms of creativity?" asks the author Njabulo Ndebele. The stranglehold of the planned monotony and rigidity has been broken. A society in transition is asserting itself. The residents of Soweto are making the city their own. They are making it liveable, they are giving it a face. What would seem like a stark, oppressive pattern from afar has a finer, more lively texture at close range. People have made space for themselves in the official grid. Soweto is not a great place to be in. It is basically flawed in many ways, and it is so by design. That is the terrifying realisation. It was constructed for a very specific purpose which it served well. It is the showcase city of apartheid's urban programme, and the scars of that strategy are visible everywhere. However, hope lies here in comparison with the 'white' suburbs around Soweto. None of this community spirit exists there. Fear has walled the suburbs in. Neighbours do not know one another. "Invest in your future! Country style Highveld living in a secure natural environment with perimeter walls topped by electric razor-wire fences, radio links to security control centres, 24hr single-entry control guardhouse, intercoms, lockable 'Hollywood' garage, eco-sensitive architectural styles, completely self-contained!" scream the opportunistic developers' advertisements.

Crime, real and brutal as it is, serves as a new business opportunity. If you can't flee the grim reality, dig in deep. We race from our Italianate palazzo-style offices in hijack-secured MRVs to the American Colonial shopping mall to our Mykonos-style suburban village. Five o'clock, change your clothes, change your lifestyle. The multiple dislocation is complete. Paranoia as principle. Cultural myopia as raison d'etre. Separate-ness on a new footing.

Cars are needed to access even the most basic provisions of daily life. Public transport in the affluent suburbs is less regular or convenient than in Soweto. And one begins to wonder whether if, after all, beneath the surface, Soweto does not carry in itself more hope for a better environment than other places such as these gated communities. People have taken control of that which was made to defeat their spirit, and are turning it around. As we leave Soweto, the silhouette of e-Goli beckons beyond the shining golden mound. Johannesburg's shadow will always be itself - but at the same time, Soweto will always be a part of Johannesburg and inseparable from its history and future.

BERLIN

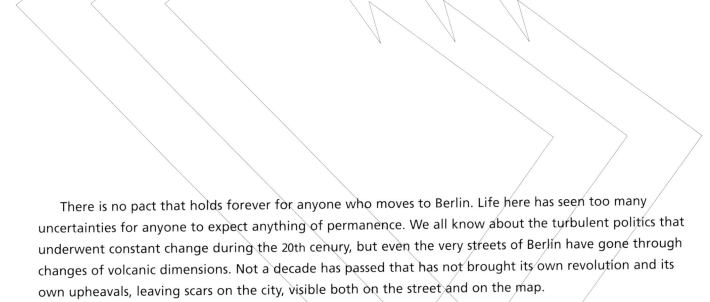

There is no pact that holds forever for anyone who moves to Berlin. Life here has seen too many uncertainties for anyone to expect anything of permanence. We all know about the turbulent politics that underwent constant change during the 20th century, but even the very streets of Berlin have gone through changes of volcanic dimensions. Not a decade has passed that has not brought its own revolution and its own upheavals, leaving scars on the city, visible both on the street and on the map.

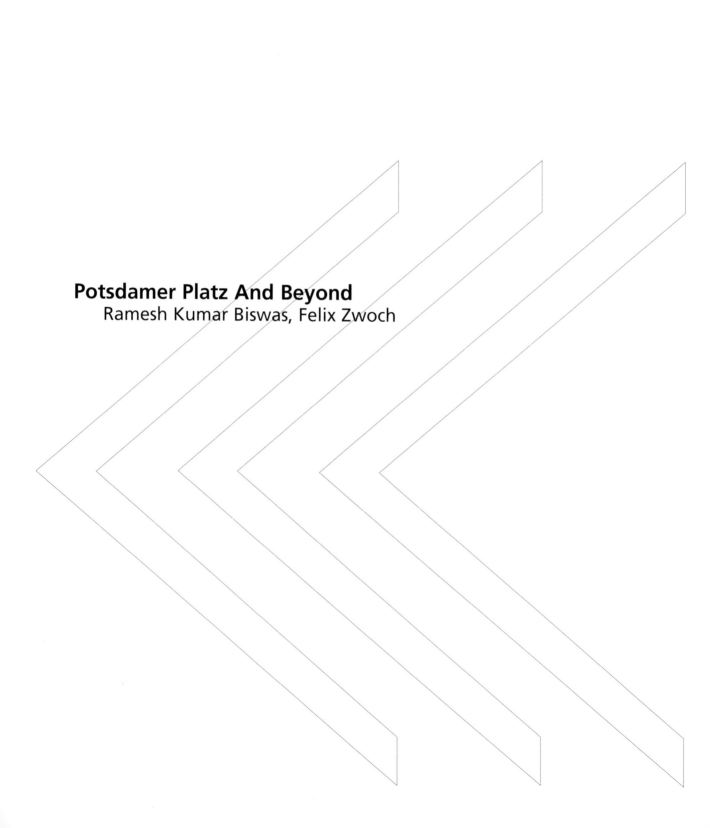

Potsdamer Platz And Beyond
Ramesh Kumar Biswas, Felix Zwoch

In 1748, Giambattista Nolli produced for the first time plans of Rome where building masses were shown in black on a white background, which represented areas without buildings. No other architectural or topographical distinctions were made, no other details interfered with this radically simplified view of the city, that enabled an unexpectedly sharp perception of its density of physical fabric and of activity. A comparison of figure/ground, black/white Nolli Plans of pre-war, post-war and post-Wall Berlin, as displayed in the catalogue 'Physiognomy of a Metropolis', shows a typically densely laid Central European urban carpet in the 30s. This structure was partially destroyed by bombing and more thoroughly decimated by bulldozers running amok during the road-building mania of the 60s and 70s, and is being repaired by new building blocks in the present time. It comes as a shock to realise that central Berlin has been almost completely demolished and rebuilt in stages during the 20th century.

BERLIN   Berlin's story during the last hundred years is so unique that if it were presented to a producer as a potential film plot it would be rejected as too far-fetched. Other cities may have also been capitals of cruel dictatorships, or destroyed by war and 1960s town planning, but none has been sliced into two in such a brutal and evident way. There would normally be no need to repeat that here was a city actually cut in half, both physically and politically, each part becoming the antipode, the antithesis of the other; each their mutual hate object, their respective bad example, each a bulwark against the other. But we do have to keep reminding ourselves of this absurd and tragic fact of history every now and then when walking through Berlin today. If there was one sentence that Ronald Reagan ever got right, it was his clear and unmistakable demand for what everyone, at the very least in retrospect, knew was right: "Tear down this wall!".

After the fall of the Wall in 1989 a period of introspection was introduced as a necessary floodgate, to halt the wild flow of speculative building that would have automatically poured over the city. The wounds had to be healed, not deepened by egoistic building that did not consider the welfare of the city as a whole. So it was not yet another bombastic monument, as architect Philip Johnson claimed the city "needed", but sheer mass to fill in the voids, as head city planner Hans Stimman established: "Berlin doesn't need new monuments, it needs a background for familiar, existing monuments. Berlin must continue to look like Berlin".

Thus the controversial, but principled approach adopted by the city's planning department, that encouraged (or forced, depending on one's standpoint) a process of "critical reconstruction". What this meant on the ground was that new developments were to recreate, at least on the street-level plan, the street/block system typical of the European city. The Modernist tenet of solitaires – individual, free-standing, expressive objects – which had led to so much fragmentation, was discarded in favour of a tightly woven, physically and multi-functionally interlinked structure of urban quarters, based on the familiar European city. It was received in Berlin as a rather courageous rule, on the borderline between progressive and reactionary.

West Berlin had already tried this approach in the International Building Exhibition (IBA) in the 80s. This was a collection of buildings specially commissioned by the city and designed by prominent architects of the time, within a tightly-knit layout meant to be programmatic and exemplary. Built around a traditional urban pattern of streets and squares and using modern (or post-modern, as the mode was then) interpretations of traditional Berlin building typologies such as the housing block and the city villa, the aim was to demonstrate a decidedly urban quality. The striving for a better quality of urban life was based on an established relationship between higher building density and social interaction on the one hand; and reduced traffic, use of land and provision of services on the other.

The policy of 'critical reconstruction' has been decried by the critic Joseph Giovannini from New York. He sees it as a means of using famous architects as fig-leaves, to beautify a strict planning principle that has led to monotonous and uniform buildings. Others were unhappy, too. Architects complained of their creativity being stifled – Daniel Libeskind, who designed the exciting new Jewish Museum, calls the city's guidelines for urban renewal authoritarian. Developers protested about not being able to maximise their sites and build high enough, investors about sliced-down profits, Berliners about the transformation of their intimate, colourful courtyards, which had become glossy, sterile and commercial. Big-city fans regret-ted the backward-looking, conservative image the controlled rebuilding was reinforcing.

The concentration on the project of 'critical reconstruction' of the centre, and the critical evaluation of this project, may also have diverted attention from the massive changes in the opposite direction on the periphery, which is steadily eating away at the image of a formerly compact city. This advantage over other European cities, dictated by the long and ugly physical barrier and the politics of four-power occupation, lasted until the fall of the Wall. Berlin had been spared a boundless urbanisation of its environs, but now the mushrooming hypermarkets and suburbs threaten to make it indistinguishable from any other urban area in Germany. The periphery has been de-urbanised, even 'provincialised', strengthening a tendency that has always existed. During the Cold War, when it enjoyed special status, thousands of young people from West Germany streamed here to escape the narrowness of their strict and unimaginative parents, their 'Wirtschaftswunder' towns and their compulsory military service. They brought their hand-knitted pullovers and Birkenstock sandals from the countryside into the former capital of cabaret and cigar smoke, 'countrifying' the metropolis. Kurt Tucholsky, the satirist, once wrote, "Berlin is a blend of the disadvantages of the big American city and of a German provincial town. Its assets can be found in the Baedecker tourist guide."

To be fair, it was not the intention of the planners to replace Modernist urban design with pre-modern approaches, or give up planning. However, it has become a case study of the limits of traditional planning. The effectiveness of the completed square and the policy behind is still being hotly debated.

But the policy was enforced with consequence and bore fruit, first along the Friedrichstrasse in the eastern part; later, on the new centre of the historic square of Potsdamer Platz, where the Wall was once most dramatically visible in a razed minefield full of fully automatic guns and soldiers. After the 'inauguration' of Potsdamer Platz in October 1998 and its near completion at the end of 2000, speculations about its quality may be tested at first hand. The myth has given way to reality. Photographers may return from their aerial lookouts to earth, and critics (that category includes almost the entire population) may now claim "I told you so", or try to find excuses for their false predictions.

Potsdamer Platz was historic also because the dramatic, Piranesian building site itself had taken on enormous symbolic significance. Busloads of people came from far-flung provinces not only to see the new centre of their new capital grow, but also to marvel at the achievements of German building technology: underwater concrete poured by divers, train tracks specially laid to handle transport to and from the site, and so on and so forth. Much has been filmed, debated and written about this new urban core, its buildings – corporate headquarters, shopping centres, a casino, a cinemax centre and a multimedia theatre – its developers, its architects, its weaknesses and the hopes invested in it. How are life and theatre in the future ever going to match the huge, decade-long performance that was the building site?

We are quite familiar with a series of Potsdamer Squares in the terrible past. The blows of fate each received gave it its specific form. Now, at the beginning of the third Millennium, at least three new squares are in the making. The first of these new Potsdamer Squares, of the impressive statistics, breathless superlatives, cubic metres, Deutsch Marks, stainless steel ferro fibre cement and underwater concrete is practically complete. Today, in continuance of the past hundred years, an extraordinary state of emergency still dominates the scene. Milling crowds throng the place, full of curiosity and hope seasoned with despair. Will this greater Berlin overcome the restrictions of its peripheral location and a troubled past, and will it resume its place as one of the most important urban centres in the world?

The aspirations of the *first* square are charged with the will to become urban and a conviction in the future of the city. Berliners expect so much of the new city that they react with cynical and suave expressions of disappointment in the results. It is, however, much too early to be either disappointed or satisfied.

The *second* new Potsdamer Platz has only now begun to move in and is steadily occupying the walls and the spaces between them. Neither town planners nor corporations have much influence on this development, a fact they are quite conscious of. Physical determinism for manipulating people through the tools of planning is no longer expected by the enlightened. A broader functional and aesthetic spectrum of variations has been established, like a coastal city at an ocean shore waiting for ships to dock. A stone has been cast into the water and the ripples are spreading outwards.

Neither the warmth of terracotta nor the gloom of granite will dominate life in the blocks here. The square is a grand technical scenography, where the skateboarder and the roller-blader, the suburbanite and the cosmopolite, the businessman and the student, the tourist from the provinces, the autonomous anarchist or the inter-rail traveller, the whore and the tramp are will move around its corridors and into its cracks and niches, covering it slowly with grime and colour, bringing it life, making it part of a real city.

By occupying every nook and cranny they will breathe into the grand square the air of notoriety and urban flair that it needs. This is the only way that the identity of the square will seep into people's consciousness, an image that will completely overlap the physical image and serve as a projection screen. Erotic aspects – Roland Barthes calls them "love and laughter" – never figure in the official calculations of city planners, yet they serve as a framework for the buildings, within which a new myth of the square and a new urban spirit can emerge. Such sensuous qualities of a square on which communication can thrive are in the making, regardless of whether the encounters are fleeting or lasting. Contrasting shades, loud voices, sinuous movements – all surface here. The whole quarter will remain *work in progress* for the next fifty years. Physical appearance will gradually have to take a back seat, to allow Potsdamer Platz to rise to the category of other metropolitan nodes such as Picadilly Circus, Shinjuku Station and Times Square, where architecture has become a natural and almost imperceptible backdrop.

One should, however, never underestimate the impact of a place's reputation. This particular square will surely feature in numerous films, television thrillers and tourist brochures. How people are going to 'see' this square, even if they never actually go there, will be the litmus test of its success. Having already achieved fame, will it also become popular? Frankly, Berlin is not typically associated with humour, congeniality or sensuality, of "love and laughter". Not that one doesn't think of it as pleasant and charming. But its history! Deadly is the word.

However, certain moments in its recent past have turned the tables. The veiling of the Reichstag by Christo, for example, put the world – and to their own surprise, even most Berliners – in an unexpectedly buoyant spirit. It was one of those moments that raise a city above its everyday cares and transports it to another plane. Another was the opening of the glass dome above the parliament in the Reichstag, enabling the people to look down upon their elected representatives in session. The unveiling of the new, completed Potsdamer Platz could become yet another moment, when long suppressed and surging emotions could find release.

Unlike the Forbidden City in imperial Beijing, a 'permitted' city is to emerge here. All indications call for optimism. The new enterprise is full of promise because so many emotions are involved and manifold hopes are concentrated in it. All major social changes are seeking expression in the new centre, in this new, better Berlin Republic, where hopefully a few new, better restaurants will come up.

"…it is proven that for Albert Einstein in 1916 the Potsdamer Platz precisely described a point in central Europe with a name on this "fixed body that is Earth", slightly shifted to the east, in the quadrant P on the map of Berlin, and served to establish the relationship between the square and the cloud floating above it, to make comprehensible and also verify 'the Specific and the General Theory of Relativity'. One could reflect on the fact that we live in a four-dimensional continuum in which time plays the same role as length, breadth and depth…", wrote Wim Wenders and Peter Handke in the book of the film 'Heaven Over Berlin'.

The *third* new square overlays the first two and is at the same time a fine network of arteries. It is not the dense flow of traffic of the thirties nor the multi-storeyed roundabout over the square in Martin Wagner's old project, but the data flowing in the 62 000 kilometres of fibreglass cables that hold the buildings together and connect them to the horizon.

The square's virtual structure also guarantees its life and, more than anywhere else, will also affect urban space. One sign for this is the bright red Info Box, a multimedia exhibition on site of all the new projects, to which public response has been enthusiastic. Colourful virtual images of the square glimmer before the construction site, which seems like a hand-coloured shot from Fritz Lang's 'Metropolis'. It would make sense to keep the Info Box in operation long after the construction has been completed, to give citizens an overview and promote interaction. After all, people even take pocket TVs with them to football matches in order to have an information edge over other fans.

The builders of the square still have no problem with the critique that the square has turned into a 'periphery in the centre of town' or into an 'island'. The reason is that, along with the conditions for town development, the rules for centrality and marginality have also changed in the competitive world of global cities. Geographical positions are transformed. Peripheral processes take place in former centres – regardless whether on a global or on an urban level. Towns can be geographically isolated in a local sense, but may function with success internationally. More than in any other place in the world this square was conceived with this idea at the back of the mind.

No one would describe the physical interface of the square with its immediate surrounding areas as entirely successful. But bits and megabytes racing about on the Infobahn need no proximity because they either extend or even replace the motion of bodies. Sophisticated debates on the city block versus experimental architectural form, therefore, will be restricted to exclusive circles. Spatial connections, which were so far a matter of course, are relaxed or even done away with, so that the elements of a densely packed conglomeration have started to dissolve and combine anew.

Regardless of whether these developments will be considered negative or positive in the future, it does not help to bury one's head in the sand. We need not fear that the city centre is about to disappear altogether because both corporate as well as non-corporate cultures still wish to intensify and concretise their activities there. Nevertheless, both internal and external organisation of space is about to change radically. Particularly the buildings on the densely cabled Potsdamer

Platz will become significantly connected – not only to their urban, but also to their cyberspace context. Once hardware and software, the power and the potential of the Web shift, the way people use it will inevitably change.

The virtual existence of a city is not limited to the commercial exploitation of communication structures. The exponential growth of Web surfers in all classes of society has turned it into a reality. The scenario becomes real when, through advanced simulation, two people, one in Munich and the other in Hong Kong, take a walk on Potsdamer Platz to meet and comment on its development, to visit an event there, to discuss and even realise a project or a business deal. Potsdamer Platz will thus become accessible to people in all parts of the world without ever having to fly there. And the ozone layer may be spared somewhat.

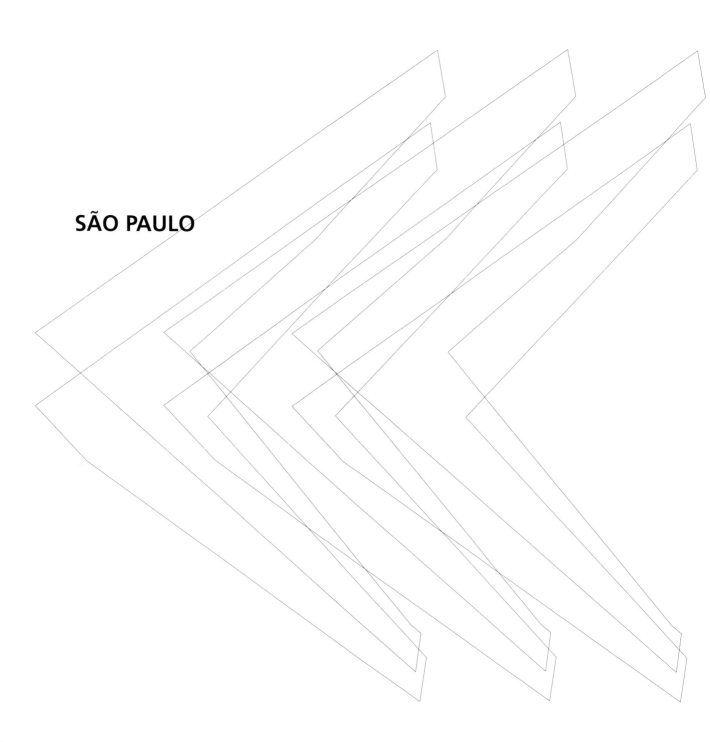

SÃO PAULO

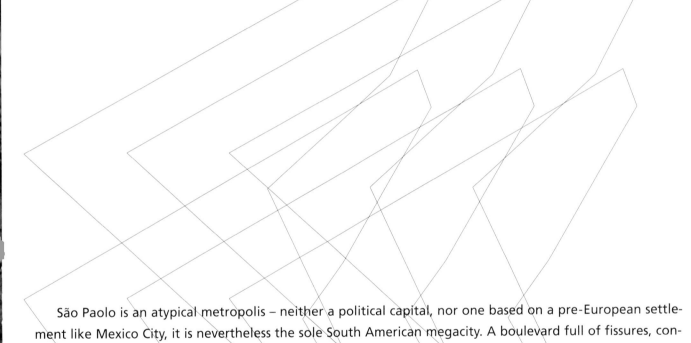

São Paolo is an atypical metropolis – neither a political capital, nor one based on a pre-European settlement like Mexico City, it is nevertheless the sole South American megacity. A boulevard full of fissures, contradictions, breaks and interruptions, the avenida Paulista is emblematic of the city it dominates.

Main Street, South America
Giselle Beiguelman

SÃO PAULO

Avenida Paulista at seven in the morning is a sight not often seen by most people. Apart from the first stirrings of sleeping people, road sweepers and night guards going home clinking their key chains, one of the busiest avenues in Latin America is still almost deserted. On weekdays, it is very quiet till 8:00 am when the rush of mini-skirted secretaries and smart-suited yuppies begins towards the offices and banks, filling the subway stations and parking lots at around 9:30. City of multiple faces, São Paulo has at avenida Paulista one of its most important centres and an emblematic urban situation of those processes of transformation.

At noon it is a kaleidoscopic panorama. Hundreds of young boys sell handmade accessories for smoking marijuana as well as incense, cheap jewellery, belts and bags. One of the biggest schools in the city is situated here, and that's the time its thousands of students occupy the street (they are privileged, as 60% of the children in the city older than 10 years are compelled to work to help their families). In the same building there are four radio and TV stations, three movie theaters and a school of journalism. Businessmen and office employees are all out on the street at lunchtime, sometimes visiting art exhibitions that take place in five cultural centres run by banks and corporate institutions. A few of them take refuge from the heat in a charming library inside the Federation of Industry.

In the evening, as well at weekends, the avenue changes a lot. Paulista shows her face as an entertainment centre, with 17 movie theatres and a gambling centre. Small bars are full, offering cheap snacks and beer. All day long unemployed people, ragged children and even a few immigrants from Western Europe walk around asking for money. The clear social hierarchy that has been entrenched for centuries has dispensed with the need for spatial segregation, as sociologist Raquel Rolnik has described in a study on urban political space. It would be a mistake to consider the avenida Paulista a miniature of the city or its metaphor. Megacities do not easily fit into this kind of box. But it is one of the powerful and dynamic images of São Paulo's contradictions and paradoxes, not just because it concentrates Latin America's main financial institutions, nor only because of its privileged geographic position, but because of its symbolic density.

São Paulo seems to have no past. It is a city of sand, shifting in continuous change. Erosion is everywhere and the ruins evoke nothing but the arbitrary nature of the real estate market. Monuments here delineate meaningless places. They lack any sense of landmark and they aren't respected for the historical events they should be symbolising. With negligible artistic attributes, they are abandoned, visited only by graffiti groups. Nevertheless, in that disavowal, they involve a desire to resist history's own tenacity.

It is a city of interruptions, disjointed, cut by rivers that made the viaducts the dominant elements of its landscape. Running on a sandy terrain of accentuated slopes, the rivers carved deep valleys and formed disconnected compartments. In São Paulo, discontinuity is the only reliable trait of continuity and urban history is also the history of barriers, of the difficulty of movement. It is a very opaque city, where topography conspires against the occupation of man. The city is in fact a network of gaps between hills, edges tacked together by underground galleries and bridges that cross invisible rivers today. A sequence of intervals, it is a shredded mess disguising nature's embarrassment in the face of concrete, and vice-versa.

A map of São Paulo looks like a quilt of remnants, cut randomly. The streets run into each other, smashing up whatever is below them. Tunnels and passages grow uncontrollably, diluting its territorial gaps. In these voids, two million people live in subhuman conditions in the '*favelas*' (sets of worker's homes roughly constructed without sanitary infrastructure, illegally built on public or private terrain) and a further 600 000 live in slums (collective habitations used by lower income people where more than four families live in a space sufficient for one).

Both *favelas* and slums as well as the increasing population of homeless people imply precarious conditions of living. Nevertheless, the very necessity of establishing different levels of deprivation reflects the degree of political violence that prevails in Brazilian society.

That is explicit in urban centers like São Paulo, where the inhabitants of the favelas constituted 1% of the population in the 70's and today represent 20% of it. It is amazing, but according to the Municipality, today more than half of São Paulo's official population of 11 million live in illegally occupied properties and 26% of their constructions lack urban infrastructure such as sewerage and electricity. São Paulo has been growing with varying speeds and in various directions since the 19th century. Divided into 96 districts, it occupies a surface of 1509 km^2 and has a demographic density of 6521 inhabitants per km^2, distributed amongst 1700 neighbourhoods and 50 000 streets.

It was described in the 30's by anthropologist Claude Lévi-Strauss in 'Tristes Tropiques' as a city impossible to figure out from a map: "It would be necessary to draw a new one every day". Prominent architect Paolo Mendes da Rocha, who has lived and built all his life in São Paulo, throws up his hands in the air when asked to comment on the city, "Impossible to illustrate this chaos!". Lévi-Strauss recorded a situation which has existed since the second half of the 19th century, more precisely the decade between 1870 and 1880. This period is assigned by historiography as the 'second founding' of São Paulo. The term gained permanence along the years, more for its conceptual accuracy than for its rhetorical impact. In that period, the triple economy of coffee, railways and immigration redefined the landscape of São Paulo and begun to reveal the strokes that characterise it now – movement, speed and agglomeration – but that did not have precedents in its history.

To have an idea of the impact of the triple economy, it is worth noting that between the founding of the city in 1554 and the inauguration of the São Paulo Railway in 1867, the city only grew negligibly. The mere one hundred inhabitants in 1554 had become a mere 31 000 in 1872. The city then had its entire process of spatial occupation redesigned on the edges of the São Paulo Railway (*Santos-Jundiaí*). This railway overcame the main obstacle to the integration of São Paulo to the colonial economy: the barrier of the Serra do Mar (the Ocean Ridge). The *Santos-Jundiaí* has linked the city, isolated by rivers and mountain ranges, to the coast. It allowed the integration of one of the only major South American cities not built on the coast with the Atlantic trade routes. It has also promoted the integration of the Tamanduateí River Bay with the city's urban perimeter, where the tracks arrive from the coast.

Until the construction of that railroad, the city's spatial entity was concentrated in the hill area, today the Pátio do Colégio, between the Anhangabaú and Tamanduateí valleys. The changes in city life that came with the trains were enormous. This forgotten old colonial village became one of the main national centres in the 1920s. It was by then growing at a rate of 14.5% a year. From the 1930s onwards, that growth rate decreased to 4,5% a year, but this was kept up till the 1980s. Today the city is still growing, but only at a rate of 0.5% per year.

In spite of that territorial spread, it is important to note that the occupation of the East side of the city transformed the Tamanduateí river, today channeled and running under avenida do Estado, into a kind of liquid wall, dividing the city socially parellel to its topography: the upper classes in the high lands around the avenida Paulista, the lower classes in the flat lands in Brás and Mooca. "Up there, they eat... down here, we work!", as the residents of Brás say. That topographic criterium was valid until at least 30 years ago, when the implantation of the subway in the East zone promoted a reconfiguration of some zones, closer to downtown, and converted it into a new real estate market for wealthy middle-class clients. Geographically, the East Zone is a flat area cut out of two swamps (that of the Tamanduateí, in its western portion, and of the Tietê, to the north) very prone to floods. Its first neighbourhood, Brás, grew dramatically in the first half of the century, and concentrated around 70% of the workforce in the textile industry, which was, until the 40s, the most significant State industrial sector.

In spite of that growth, frequent floods troubled the East Zone, and still do so, exposing the almost schizophrenic fashion in which the integration of this neighbourhood took place. This relationship of disintegrated integration continues till today. Unrestrained growth continued until World War II. From then onwards, there was a decrease in the neighbourhood's population. Many factors contributed to that: the implantation of highways that created new industrial areas alongside the Anchieta and Anhangüera highways; and the technological and business management transformations that, beginning with World War II, have fundamentally modified textile production, leading to the obsolescence of the textile plants that have dominated the Brás landscape.

Moreover, in the 1950s, the Plan of Purposes encouraged the production of durable goods and the massive influx of foreign resources to areas outside the city, giving a different industrial profile to the State of São Paulo. Population increased by 65% in the outer areas in the 1960s alone, but then decreased in the centre, reflecting the displacement of low-income classes to peripheral districts with lower rents, pushing poverty, prostitution and political unrest further to the East, 50 km away from downtown. There the demographic rate of increase has reached 11% in the last ten years in contrast to the decrease of around 4.5% in the same period in the old East Zone, located 6 km from downtown São Paulo. It is the new periphery that is now attracting migrants in spite of its miserable infrastructure and urban services.

The military dictatorship initiated several urban planning schemes from 1964 onwards. Between the old industrial centre (closer to downtown) and those new peripheral districts, middle-class neighbourhoods emerged recently after the completion of the subway, since it was parallel to the opening of new avenues and viaducts that favoured vertical growth and revaluation on the real estate market.

Another fact directly linked to that process of change, speeded by the construction of the subway in the old industrial zone, is more political in nature. For the subway construction a 26-hectare area was declared of public utility and more than 900 buildings were razed there. The plan of reoccupation of the area presumed the construction of new housing, schools, churches and day-care centres for the low-income population.

Nevertheless, this plan for the reoccupation of the demolished area was only put forth between 1986 and 1987, in the last administration of mayor Jânio Quadros. It resulted in the construction by the State of countless identical, frightful housing blocks along the subway line from Brás to Belenzinho. The promised day-care centres, schools, and churches were left out. "Night life?" snorts Mendes da Rocha when asked about what people do here after work, "Night death is more like it." As a consequence, that portion of the city became a large territorial gap and an example of the close relationship between big contractors, large public services enterprises and politicians.

This situation has been a constant since 1900, when the country entered the Republican period, but not with the same cast. From 1900 to World War II, the "joint venture" was between the coffee planters and British public enterprises and banks, such as the São Paulo Railway and Lloyds Bank. From World War II till the 80's the power over the city was formed out of the combination of multinational enterprises and (mostly North American) financial institutions, allied to emergent politicians, some of them strongly linked to the military dictatorship that governed the country from 1964 to the 1980s. Industrial production doubled within the 50 years to 1970, income increased by 4.5% per decade. Since the 1980s, production in some sectors has gone down by 40%. The military emphasised urban planning as a centralised power tool which diverted attention from its illegitimacy, as the geographer Andreas Novy notes, "De-politicised experts were put in charge. The "sick" city was treated as a machine to be repaired, just as the sick human being has been treated by modern medicine." Of course this approach failed, especially as the experts were not allowed to implement anything that might threaten the regime.

From then onwards the changes were deeply related to globalisation and transnational economies. The city completely lost its traditional forms of spatial organisation. On the one hand there was the emergence of new areas of construction which have incorporated areas that did not exist a few years ago. On the other, illegal occupation increased tremendously, extending the city limits. The "parachuteros" were arriving in streams from the countryside to set up new slums and find work. The rigid class division within the occupation patterns imploded, and poverty and misery are omnipresent today. New security systems have been systematically adopted, converting the city into several walled cells, where violence and fear constitute dominant architectural elements and reconfigure social exclusion in urban space.

São Paulo has not had an urban master plan since the military regime's plans of 1972, in spite of the fact that sporadic initiatives periodically course up and down the corridors of government. At the beginning of the 1990's, for instance, the first portion of the East zone was symbolically integrated to the city, when mayor Luiza Erundina from the Workers' Party (a mass church-supported movement of the landless and the urban poor), the first woman to occupy this office, transferred the Town Hall from the aristocratic quarter of Ibirapuera to the proletarian Brás neighborhood, that is now, at least, equipped with easy access by public transportation. Certain urban highways were closed on Sundays to be occupied by football-kicking youths and families grilling at impromptu stands. For four years, civil society merged with local administration, to try to establish a decentralised and citizen-oriented urban planning process that has since been reversed by subsequent conservative administrations.

The changes under mayor Erundina may have been an icon of the city's first left-wing administration, but had little influence on the neighbourhood's urban reshaping. The gap between the rich and the poor increased. 25% of the inhabitants earn 5.8% of the total income, whereas the upper 25% earn 61.4% (Barelli/Dedecca 1989). The landscape is today dominated by collective housing, empty properties and abandoned industrial structures, seamed by dull recent development. Simultaneously, between the 70's and the 90's, the city lost that strong logic of clear social divisions and precise borders. Illustrative of this process is the avenida Paulista. At an elevation of 800 metres, the avenue contrasts with the rest of the city's topography. It projects itself sideways, upwards and downwards, dividing the city into its main parts. Southwards and towards the southwest, the terrain goes down, searching out the Pinheiros River. Northwards and eastwards, it goes down in an accentuated slope, going after the Tietê and Tamanduateí Rivers.

A centennial boulevard, it has been a synonym for power from its beginning in 1891, when it enjoyed the status of being the widest avenue of the city, with three dirt lanes: one for animal drawn trolleys, the second for ox carts, and the third for horsemen. From 1900 to the 1960s it was an exclusive residential area, lined with the mansions of plantation owners who had diversified into industry, banking, trade and, logically, politics at an early stage and who needed an urban presence, as economists Wilson Cano and Leonardo Neto have documented. For centuries before, it was merely the Caaguassu, which in the Tupi language means 'big jungle', something that sounds strangely appropriate looking at the landscape of the avenue today.

Portugal did not encourage the development of a local urban bourgeoisie which might have become a political challenge, and hence an independent urban cultural life was throttled. For centuries the avenue only served the troops of Santo Amaro – now in the south of the city – as a route to the slaughter house. It was urbanised by an Uruguayan businessman, Joaquim Eugenio de Lima, who bought the land on both sides of the road. The few constructions of the early 20th century seem to be haunted by their history. They are architectural moments of a city beginning to industrialise, to build up its infrastructure and to organise non-African immigration into the city with the help of excess capital generated by the expanding coffee plantations, foreign loans and new laws cementing private urban property rights. Fruit of a very successful real estate enterprise (it is still the most expensive area of São Paulo), the avenue exhibits in its very name the signs of the transformation of the city's political and economic role: a *Paulistano* is a person who was born in the city of São Paulo, whereas a *Paulista* is someone who was born in the State of São Paulo. The amount of power concentrated there made the avenue the embodiment of the power of the State in the 20th century. With its large mansions and its floral sidewalks, it used to be the perfect expression of the influential position of the agrarian and the industrial bourgeoisie. It is the use of the financial surplus for the development of a local market and sound investment, instead of wasteful luxury consumption, that the economist Celso Furtado sees as the reason for its rise and consolidation. It has, however, changed a lot in the last 30 years.

An urban reform plan in 1968 enlarged its roads to a width of 48 metres and opened a tunnel under it, converting it into a beautiful two level avenue. By that time, its first business buildings had been erected and the Museum of São Paulo (MASP) was inaugurated. Old downtown São Paulo, where the older financial and cultural institutions as well its earlier entertainment centers were concentrated, gradually lost its traditional functions. At the same time avenida Paulista became more complex and incorporated the anxieties and contradictions of the late modernism of the 60s. That doesn't mean the avenue lost its gentrified mood, but since then it became one of the most important financial centres of Latin America. Its role as a service centre was strengthened, implying a shift toward social miscegenation, but not the democratisation of its space. As a matter of fact, one of the most curious things about São Paulo is that there are no formal public spaces. Every corner seems to be irrelevant to its past, present or future. And in this sense, too, the avenida Paulista, through which half a million people pass every day, is symbolic.

Along its three kilometres, the avenue shelters not only the headquarters of North American, European, Latin American and national banks and enterprises, chambers of commerce, multinational trade operations and exchange houses, but also radio and TV stations and an important hospital and educational complex. All the largest private banks have their headquarters here. The avenue houses, not by chance, many influential consulates and ministries. It is the address of powerful national syndicates and corporate institutions like the FIESP (Federation of the Industries of the State of São Paulo) and the SESC (Social Services of Commerce).

Nevertheless, this commercial dominance and suppression of the vision of the city could not prevent the recent proliferation of free theatres, art galleries and good multimedia labs at the banks and corporate institutions that has converted the avenida Paulista into the city's main cultural core. One of the few architectural masterpieces of the city, the Museum of São Paulo, is also located here. Designed in 1956 by the architect Lina Bo, the site had been donated by the municipality to its founder,

Assis Chateaubriand, a kind of tropical Citizen Kane, on the condition that the views to the centre of the city were to remain unobstructed. The central idea of the Bo project was to preserve these sight lines, creating a unique building with four 70 metre-high pillars holding up the main body, with two subsoil floors and two floors above ground level. Since 1997 this void has been blocked by a privately built insertion. In spite of the serious visual damage to the landscape, the blocking-off of this space is meaningful to the debate on the imprecision of the borders between the spheres of private and public space. It is undeniable that this imprecision translates other political weaknesses which, in turn, exhibit historical scars of colonial exploitation, slavery and frequent periods of dictatorship, linked to the country as well as to Latin America as a whole. The suppression of the city view points to a curious inversion: what should be public becomes private and hidden. What is private shows up as public, hiding its mechanisms of selection. Even all those galleries, theaters and libraries exclude people through intimidation. With their armed guards and heavy-money atmosphere – do not forget that all of them occupy marbled bank foyers and corporate halls that intimidate and select who is and who is not an insider of the system, through their own primary function (to protect money).

It stresses the peculiarities of the privatisation of culture in São Paulo, which find an interesting parallel in the transformation of the famous void of the MASP building into a kind of monumentalisation of public space converted into ruins. Increasingly, ruins of dirty fences are appearing on empty and demolished sites here, announcing epileptic landscapes, where now besides the Faustian bank and corporate buildings there is a huge shopping centre that only deals in pirated software and illegal imported electronic goods. In this sense the MASP building becomes an evidence of the curious movement of temporal suspension that seems to define this city and to link its dynamics to the desertification of the industrial zone. Formerly Latin America's leading industrial centre, São Paulo City now concentrates the telecommunications market within it. The city shelters half of Brazil's 200 largest technology enterprises and a further 829 software enterprises. In comparison, Rio de Janeiro, the second Brazilian New Economy market, holds only 369 software enterprises.

But the New Economy centre is gradually shifting far away from avenida Paulista as well as from the entire traditional central area. It occupies a recently urbanised region, beside the Pinheiros river in the western portion of the city, in the exclusive Berrini avenue, where "exclusive" means the exclusion of any activity that does not have "techno-" as a prefix. There is no public space here worth mentioning.

The creeping ruins of avenida Paulista can be read, then, as more than merely abandoned places. They are the exposed scars of a lost physiognomy. Its decadence does not display any indication of transformation. Quite the contrary – what prevails here is the same absence so deeply felt in the old industrial areas and in downtown. A suspension of the orientations of present, past and future, a gesture of the draining of history, in a continuous state of transition toward nothing.

MOSCOW

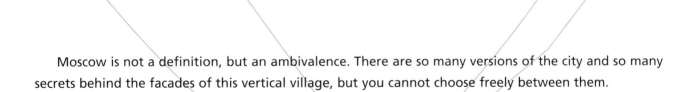

Moscow is not a definition, but an ambivalence. There are so many versions of the city and so many secrets behind the facades of this vertical village, but you cannot choose freely between them.

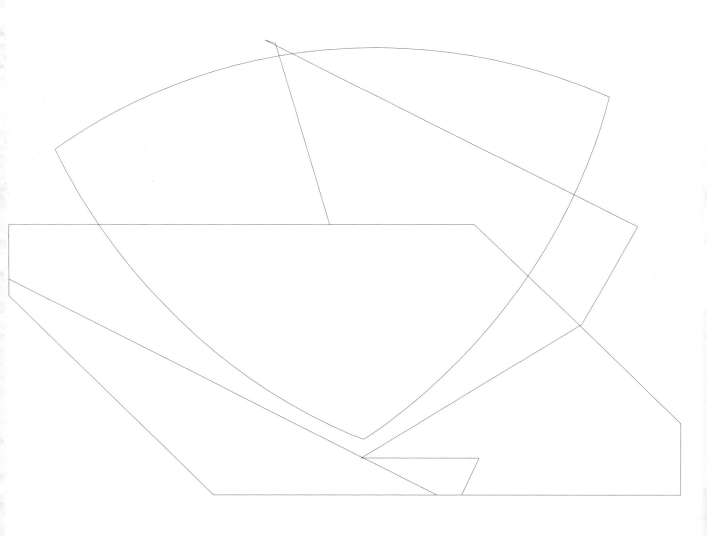

Hotel Moskva

Felix Zwoch

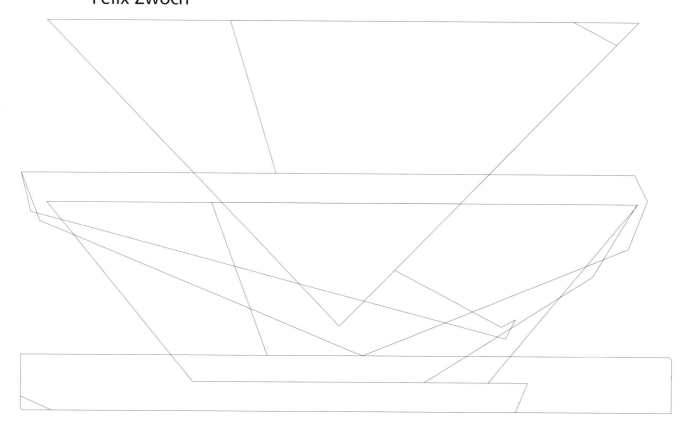

MOSCOW

That I was going to book a room in the Hotel Moskva on this last visit was a foregone conclusion, and I was undeterred by all the difficulties to come. After several phone calls, Helios, my travel agent in Berlin, had to put pressure on the Olympia travel agency in Cologne who asked for my passport, which eventually came back with a very picturesque visa stamped on it. My name was spelt in three different ways: Zwoch, ЦBOX, Cvoch. So I travelled to Moscow under three different names and stayed in a plush red-velvet-lined room behind the graceful facade of the ten-storeyed hotel on the Manege Square. It was built by Alexei V. Shtyusev, the 1920s architect who also built the Lenin Mausoleum and the Lenin Library, about whom I yearned to learn more.

When I arrived in Moscow, it was pretty busy dealing with a series of spectacular Mafia murders and less spectacular muggings of foreign visitors; with miserable, cold, wet, aching weather; and with a traffic collapse due to several, complicated infrastructural difficulties, all at the same time. Intensely passionate and depressing, the city is its own obvious explanation for its high vodka consumption. I looked out of the window into a grey, depressing soup enveloping grey, painful buildings, I saw drunks weaving through little groups of uniformed men and prostitutes on the square, and I decided to stay put for the moment in my warm, dry room. I asked everyone who could tell me something about Moscow to come and see me in the Hotel Moskva, where it had been so difficult to get a room, and they were all quite pleased to come.

I love this hotel's Stalinist neo-classicist façade. Built almost symmetrically on either side of an axis, it has apparently whimsical aberrations. Departing from strict symmetry, it appears partially mirrored but partially transformed. With architectural inventiveness, Shtyusev flanked the tall centre with two side wings. While base, centre and eaves are organised identically, the cornices and windows of these two wings, which should, according to the rules of neo-classical Moscow architecture be mirror images, are actually varied. Popular belief has it that the façade was not really designed by Shtyusev. In reality, both his drawing and that of another architect who was well-versed in symmetrical axis architecture just happened to be on Stalin's desk. They say that Stalin, who in his characteristically touching manner always insisted on granting personal permission for buildings with such great urban impact, signed them both by mistake. Solomonic judgement, nobody knows whose, led to both façades being built – one to the right of the symmetrical axis and the other to the left of it. Stalin's interest was by no means Solomonic, says yet another legend which, though even more absurd, is the more plausible of the two. It is said that two ambitious foremen, vying for speed, meddled about with two drawings. Though the drawings were almost identical, one foreman held his drawing upside down and read the cornice as the base. This seems to be the only logical explanation for the shift in detail and the strangely similar aberrations. Yet another story that stems from this one seems to confirm or even fortify this interpretation. Rumour has it that not two but three foremen lie buried in the foundations of the famous hotel. What crime they were guilty of never became known. "Enough, enough of architects' yarns," I cried finally when the fourth story was unrolled. But each of my guests in the hotel lobby adamantly stuck to his own version. Politely they ate their caviar on toast and drank their beer – served in this famous place for 20 Roubles, less than one Euro, though they cost twice as much elsewhere in Moscow. I asked myself if the legends would have seemed equally plausible to me had I not heard them within the confines of the austere, white marble lobby. Would they have rung quite as true had they been told me in the enormous stuccoed, ornate-pillared, velvet-curtained and gilded dining room? But that room, the symmetrical element that projects from the famous façade above the sealed main entrance, has been chained, padlocked and closed to the public. Probably some more foremen in there.

Later in the evening, a uniformed and liveried giant – clearly a person of considerable importance – came to our table and ordered my Russian guests to leave. This hotel is exclusively for foreign guests, he explained. He was not responsible for rebuttals or protestations. I rushed over to the reception desk. The people there, too, were not responsible. But the representatives of Intourist in the back room were. I rushed there. The Intourist counter, however, was closed and had been closed since six o'clock, as usual. So I returned to the round table of fables of the city, each version its own reference. In the long decades of suppressed information, rumours replaced truth as the genuine experience of Moscow, and habits die hard.

During my absence, a fifth story about the façade's design had been related. I made them repeat it. According to first-hand information, Shtyusev's authorship of the façade was never proven and is a falsification of history. An unknown architect to whom acclaim was denied all his life was the one who had designed this unique façade. Now in his early nineties, he apparently lives somewhere in the depths of the hotel's cellars and catacombs that connect to the Kremlin and several other places of political significance to the former regime. Compassionate people working in the makeshift kitchens, now found on practically all floors of the hotel, who helpfully point out new guests to prostitutes for a commission, provide him with food and drink and place them on the same spot everyday. Nobody has seen him for a long time, but the plates and glasses are always found empty in the morning.

One of my group of local experts on the city, the slightly older one, the professor, was a bit restless during the telling of these stories, but he remained silent. While we were saying our goodbyes at the swinging doors, however, he said something to the doorman in a low voice. He wanted to know whether he had permission to enter the hotel at all... "But you were, you still are, you're coming straight from..." – all to no avail. Didn't hotel regulations refuse him entry to it? he demanded insistently. Wasn't it quite clear that the hotel was only meant for foreign guests, and that he, merely a Moscow architect, had no right to be there? The comrade doorman could, indeed, *should* have intervened. The doorman simply shrugged his shoulders, nodded, pacified. This was the year 2000, after all. But he was absolutely certain, said the architect.

Moscow cannot be described on the same terms as other European cities. Is there a Moscow identity, and if so, where could I look for it? On the Red Square, in the Metro, in the prefab housing slabs on the periphery, in the Orthodox churches, the Art

Nouveau palaces or the Stalinist wedding-cake monstrosities? My next visitor was the erudite urbanist Dieter Hoffmann-Axthelm, who told me a lot about the urban structure of Moscow and the power of images. Of Moscow as the one place in the whole world where archaic and global codes interact violently, unchecked, as a continuum of the past – and not because the very old and the very new fuse as in Asian cities. Today's Moscow deals with rumours, images and untruths in a unique way. "The city seems to have no problem whatsoever with all this. Moscow is exploding with impertinent symbols. Its newly acquired wealth is visible everywhere, as visible in the freshly gilded church dome in the heart of the city as it is in the unimpeded disintegration caused by a wildly expansive growth. This is as comforting as the fatalistic restorative activity of its subjects, which must necessarily replace the lack of a beneficial civil structure between this very symbolic dome, on the one hand, and the outright struggle for survival on the other.

One immediately notices this other aspect of Moscow on stepping outside the Garden Ring. The closer one looks at it the more sharply does the reality of life for the majority of its inhabitants become delineated. Ostensible security regulations enforced by the police are as much a part of it as the imperceptible exclusion of the outside world. Moscow is a closed city, not hermetically but effectively. The loopholes (behind every guarded entrance there is always an unguarded one, even at the rail terminals that are essentially border crossing points) are perhaps left there on purpose. Getting caught without a permit during a routine check, one reads in the Moscow Times, means contributing heavily towards financing the enterprise that is Moscow.

Without actually being one itself, Moscow has its share of Third World city violence. When compared to cities like Riga, Wilna, Warsaw, Krakow, Prague, Bratislava or Budapest, Moscow is Eastern European only in a limited sense. Its basic structure, however, is essentially that of an Asian city. What differentiates it from both European as well as Asian cities is the comprehensive urban iconography. In Europe, structure comprises images as well as the applied executive power of the state. In Asia, on the other hand, one does not interfere with the emerging functional mass.

In my view, the issue is not the city, the issue is Moscow. While the bourgeois lifestyle of the city is nothing, the autocratic national manifestation is everything. Just this one city exists, not several small, medium, or very large cities based on a common model. Moscow, therefore, is not a proper name but the name of a species. All the various and ambivalent definitions from the past seem to underline this aspect: *gorod* is the ambivalence between city and fort, *posad* between small town and suburb, *kreml* between castle and enclosed square, *sloboda* between the market and every other free space. The list could be extended still further. Typological analysis cannot be separated from political preconditions, and precisely herein lies the task of reading the typology, the ground plan of the city in a social, a political way.

The squares as well as anarchic open spaces in the city, such as those in front of the Belorussian railway station or the highly stylised Mayakovsky Square can be seen in the context of Moscow's hierarchical social centres. There are other places and spectacular new plazas such as the Raskovoi Square, where Leningrad Prospect bifurcates into Leningrad Chausee and Wolokolamska Chausee, or Leningrad Prospect and the Railway Ring intersect at Gagarin Square, that all belong to the same genre. It is not a question of the type of square, it is about the essence of meaning. A presence, so to speak, a requisitioned, conscious, social presence – regardless of whether it is needed or used, full of life or simply filled. Seen in this context, it is not liberal public space but social space. It is not a proposal but a proclamation.

The rift between city and countryside becomes distinct when compared to the enormous, yet not illuminated hinterland. Here, the real junctions of public services – modelled after subway entrances and market halls or similar infrastructural centres – clusters of market stalls, mobile shops, people waiting, eating or drinking all merge to present an entirely different, oriental street life.

The presence of the village in the city and, to a certain extent, of the forest in the city: the structure of both these derivative forms can still be discerned, not in a literal sense but in the context of the city centre. Moscow's centre has become sedentary, inflexible and permanent. The reason why this fusion of rural and urban has become a singular entity is because the displaced – the village, the forest – has taken over the developed. Whether five, ten or fourteen-storeyed, the houses do not stand a

chance against the power of this other life, slowly taking over. The very way the inhabitants move around the area and amble casually in the middle of mire-seamed and rutted streets reflects a defiance of established structures. Endless wobbly fences, containers lined up at some intersection or the other, demobilised vehicles and garages adapted to function as shops or workshops where people sell, build, cook, eat, drink or do their office work – all of these demonstrate the return of what rigid modern structures no longer allow and attempt to banish forever."

Finally I had to step out of the Hotel Moskva. Grey figures hurried along grey facades, seemingly fleeing the end of time. Fat *babushkas* and sensationally beautiful young girls waited next to each other in the Metro stations. Armed with maps and a few friends, I searched for the city beyond the picture-postcard centre that manages to fulfill every tourist's high expectations with the greatest of ease. We went to see the massive prefabricated housing blocks that make up the real world of Moscow, where most of the residents (or their parents) could be assumed to have been denunciators. The more colleagues they denounced, the bigger the flats allocated to them, unless and until the day came when they themselves were denounced. These enormous blocks of flats (no deviations from symmetry here) were a direct result of Kruschev's decrees in the autumn of 1955 that forbade the wasteful excesses of Stalinist decorative architecture and ordered stringency of form, simplicity and economy based on industrialised building systems. In the East as in the West, capital-intensive construction was meant to make 'modern' flats affordable to the workers, something it achieved here beyond the dreams of pre-war modernists. Now the biting wind of the steppes whistles through the cracks between the panels, vodka bottles are being consumed, wives battered and minor gangsters murdered in the stairways. But the post-modern 'native' style now being propagated as a counter-strategy to the soulless modernism of the past is no more than monumental kitsch, almost as depressing.

We went to look for Viktor Melnikov's house. Melnikov, a visionary Constructivist architect who built the Russian Pavilion at the Paris World Fair of 1925, as well as the famous cubist Rusakova Worker's Club, was later persecuted, banned to Saratov and forbidden to build or teach for decades. The house – a leaky ruin; its contents – remnants of drawings and notes looked after as well as possible by his impoverished 85 year-old son – a monument to wasted talent and suppressed potential. This is a city, remarked one of my companions, the writer Helmut Frauendorfer, that is merciless to its citizens, who are in turn merciless to it.

I returned to my room in the Hotel Moskva. I looked out of my window at the grey city, with the pinnacles of Moscow University stabbing at the winter sky out of the heavy fog. As Hoffmann-Axthelm said finally, it is impossible to identify with Moscow. Everything else, whether fascination, love, disgust, sympathy, or awe is up to you. In my desire to stay in my room in the Hotel Moskva and block out the street, I found I was in good company when I picked up the emigré author Sinoviy Sinik's book, "The Horror Story of Emigration", and read the following passage, "The geography of the street in the Russian novel is full of gaps, both literally and metaphorically. Descriptions of the street are extremely rare…In the Russian novel, people do not meet on the street, but in a weather zone: of frost, of thaw, of summer heat or of the clear autumn; they come together to discuss the cosmic problems of the Russian *intelligenziya*: for what price and where one could buy a bottle and quickly visit another house, a shop, a flat; then, finally, begins the description of everyday life, of events, of faces, of furniture, of pictures. Between these transit stations lie the empty spaces of the city, black holes of existence. The city itself has no topography, it exists only as isolated neighbourhoods and houses, in which we satisfy our small passions in the company of friends."

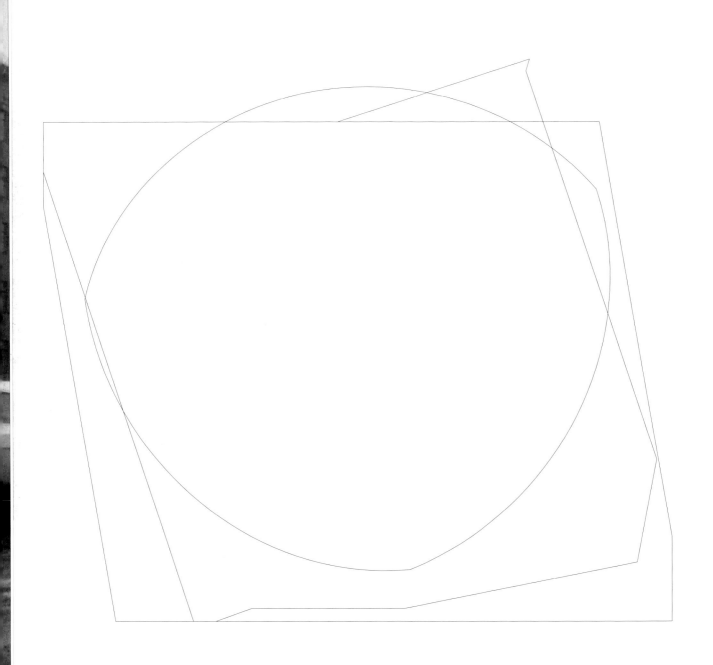

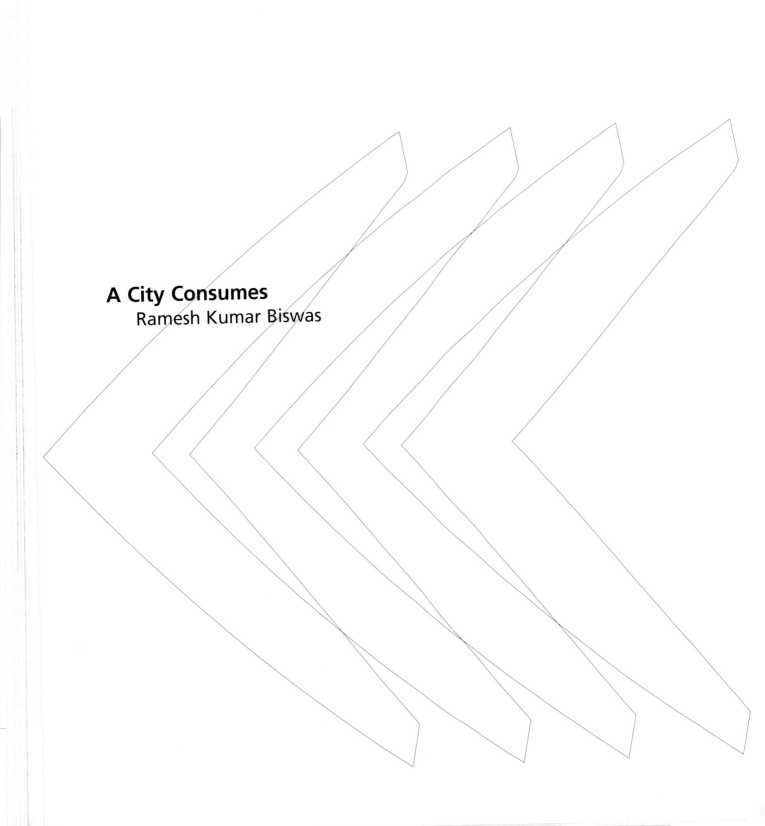

A City Consumes
Ramesh Kumar Biswas

A City Consumes
Ramesh Kumar Biswas

For if there were a twist to a tale, Vienna would provide it. If there is a back door to slip out through, Vienna is not the city to miss it. If a city could have a second name, Ambiguity would be Vienna's. Behind everything that you see here are layers of complexities (and complexes, to boot).

Vienna may not be the "experimental arena for the end of the world" as its fierce critic and chronicler Karl Kraus called it in the 30s, but it may well be a laboratory for consumerism. Not that it is a "sell, sell, sell" city like Taipeh or New York, but it is a place where 20th century society has taken major steps towards a conscious exploitation of elements of modern existence – food, cultures, time, radicalism, the subconscious mind. Let us, then, slit open some tightly sealed and beribboned packages and look at their contents. Let us look at how Vienna consumes, to understand the way it is. Many things that began here as little ideas have found their way, on a different scale, to other places, with not-so-pleasant consequences.

VIENNA

The first example that springs to the mind is the Karl Marx Hof, the famous social housing complex one endless kilometre long, built in the 1920s to alleviate the miserable living conditions of migrant workers from the far flung corners of the Austro-Hungarian monarchy. Photographs exist of people at the beginning of the 20th century who had to sleep in cellars and sewers. Workers had to share beds in shifts in tiny flats. The Socialist Party that won elections to the town council in 1919 started an ambitious programme of new housing for workers, with running water in the flats and communal amenities like kindergartens and laundries. Several housing blocks were built, comparable in size to the flagship Karl Marx Hof. This unique achievement of the city council of "Red Vienna" was financed by a housing tax levied on the upper and the middle classes. The projects restructured large parts of the city due to their sheer size and urban design impact, but they did not lose a sense of human scale designed as they were around pleasant green courts. Once this idea was transported over the border, however, and later over the English Channel and the Atlantic, it took the form of gigantic housing blocks that inevitably degenerated. In the view of linguist Marshall Berman, the erection of vast housing estates in New York was a direct ideological import from Vienna's social housing programme, but their omission of communal facilities ultimately contributed to their decline into unmanageable slums.

A closer look at this programme reveals elements significant to the future of consumer society. Since it was not solely a social programme but also a political manifesto, tenants were selected whose political leanings were not a hundred miles away from the Socialist Party. The very inauguration of the Karl Marx Hof was an early *mise en scène* of political management of the masses. Life in these 'castles' was a precursor of a totalitarian Modernist planning later applied in different degrees to housing in the US, France and the USSR.

They turned their back to the city, and concentrated community life in an introverted environment. A crucial element was the steering of consumer patterns. Club life was emphasised in every sphere – organised by trade unions, party-affiliated children's and youth organisations, sport and cultural associations; and above all, the consumer association appropriately named 'Konsum'. Co-operative Konsum supermarkets in the housing complexes were meant not only to provide the tenants with goods, but also to build up an alternative power field to the city's bourgeois shop-keepers. The Konsum empire grew into an influential political factor until its bankruptcy in 1995. Thus, perversely enough, the emergence of organised consumerism and of the supermarket in Vienna was socialist-inspired rather than being a product of capitalism.

Another misunderstood export, arising from social changes in households – smaller families, no household staff – was the famous 'Frankfurt kitchen' of the 1920s. Though not made in Vienna itself, it was designed by the Viennese architect Margarethe Schütte-Lihotzky, and reflected a typical Viennese preoccupation with the small scale. A prefabricated, rational and ergonomically planned kitchen that was meant to reduce the chores of cooking and release women from drudgery, it suffered the fate of all Viennese inventions. Adopted by industry and installed as uniform, non-ergonomic fitted kitchens in practically every household, they have been responsible for degrading the lady of the house to a housewife, isolating her from the family and compensating her loneliness by consumer products and kitchen appliances. The standardisation of the kitchen went hand in hand with that of food itself.

With regard to packaging, transport and storage norms, food was for the first time quantified in terms of size and weight. This standardisation demanded centralised production, highways and supermarkets at the expense of small groceries, butchers and market stands.

Consumer behaviour is one of the most determining structural influences on a city. It is of crucial importance if economic activities are concentrated in large units or if they are accessible in decentral, small units. A dispersed, small-scale commercial infrastructure creates local activities in the street and corresponds to specific needs. There are few large cities in Europe that offer a comparable network of small shops. This is a non-formal element that dominates the street scene in Vienna and makes it lively – a result of imperial commercial laws that permitted each shop to only sell one type of product. A hat maker was not allowed to sell coats, and a greengrocer could not offer his customers nuts and bolts. These regulations, strictly observed until the middle of the 19th century and only gradually undermined in the course of time, influenced the distribution of goods and services.

The supermarket is a unit that can be reached by foot; it is integrated in the neighbourhood. The next stage, the hypermarket or the shopping mall on a green field site, no longer has a functional connection to it. The Shopping City Süd, a shopping mall and hypermarket jumble outside the city limits, with 29 million customers and a turnover of a billion Euro annually, is Europe's biggest shopping centre. Such air-conditioned and 'pedestrian-friendly' malls, friendly only to pedestrians who can drive there by car, are yet another example of those brilliant and original Viennese inventions that are now disfiguring the world. It was an *emigré* Viennese architect, Victor Gruen, who wanted to do something to counteract the decline of inner-city areas in the US. He created the first shopping malls, meant to provide attractive and safe consumer/leisure zones. His first shopping centres contained community facilities and were served by public transport. As this idea was enthusiastically taken up and blown up tenfold by speculative developers, they eliminated small shops in the city centre and produced massive vehicular traffic, noise, pollution and waste of energy. The Shopping City Süd is a magnet for 50 000 cars a day, which transform the entire area into a permanent traffic jam that fire engines and ambulances find hard to penetrate. There have been several inventive robbers who have fled from the Shopping City on motorcycles, which police cars were unable to pursue.

Shortsighted regional politicians, blinded by astronomical tax revenues, are promoting the construction of similar malls all around Vienna. The 4300-soul village of Vösendorf, which hosts the Shopping City, is the richest local authority in Austria. In spite of having money to burn – the tiny village has two swimming halls – the residents are fed up of traffic jams and accidents, and are opposing an expansion. Politicians in the capital, who have lost billions in tax revenues, briefly considered supporting competing shopping malls on Viennese land. However, massive resistance within City Hall, from experts and from local businesses made them drop the idea. Present policy supports the retention of small-scale infrastructure in the city.

Here's interesting news for opponents of state intervention in commerce: this policy works. Today 80% of consumer expenditure is still within one's own district – highly beneficial for small shopkeepers. It is an example of how an organised coalition of small-scale commerce and a proactive city administration have managed to avoid the emptying of central districts common elsewhere. The clientele of the Shopping City has also changed. It now mostly serves customers from rural regions who come there for a breath of urbanity. Residents of Vienna, who have urbanity at first hand, now prefer to stay in the important shopping streets of the city, with their mix of luxury boutiques and low-budget stores. The attractiveness of the inner city – a consequence of the attention given to the architectural design of shops with their luxurious materials, exclusive design and witty window displays that often do not show the wares actually on sale – are preferred by the consumer. In this aspect, Vienna has pre-empted the new consumer trends, in which goods themselves are less important than the message they convey. The postmodern consumer does not necessarily need the wares he buys, but he buys them nonetheless for pleasure, prestige or out of sheer frustration.

One of the consequences of overcrowding during the *Gründerzeit* since 1873 – the period of initial industrialisation and large-scale property speculation – was the emergence of cheap little eating places and soup kitchens on almost every street corner. The historian Siegfried Mattl, analysing present society in the light of past living conditions, notes that until 1880, with the exception of the homes of the aristocracy or the *grand bourgeoisie*, there were few kitchens in the crowded flats. Work patterns were unique, too. The way people in Vienna work, even today, is rather relaxed and quite the opposite of strictly disciplined – how it has become one of the richest cities in the world is an obscure mystery even to its finance minister. The existence of so many small craftsmen, who worked long hours but mixed work with social activities and frequent breaks for food – people enjoyed a second breakfast and an afternoon snack, making five meals a day – supported numerous small cafés and so-called 'Beisl', a sort of pub, that were open most of the day and night. To this day, inexpensive *plats du jour* are affordable and cheaper than cooking at home. The later development of regulated factory and office hours with fixed lunch breaks led to shorter opening hours and finally to the closure of many of these small localities.

The Beisl, where the unemployed, the student, the tattooed small-time (or even the big-time) crook, card-tricksters, thrifty pensioners, drunks and tired whores spent their time, is still around. It is not an exclusive institution. A construction worker and a doctor may be regulars of the same Beisl. Here, too, Vienna has been a precursor of postmodern consumerism. Unlike in a conventional restaurant in England or the US, where you are served the bill the moment you finish eating, in Vienna you may sit for hours over a beer or a coffee, and no one would dream of throwing you out. That is, the material worth of what is on offer is less important than the symbolic value, the ambience, the social communication, the experience. This trend is now creeping into new museum-restaurants in England and Germany, where people go to see and be seen, and to be part of the scene, rather than for the food.

The better class of Beisl is being supported by low-interest modernisation loans and subsidies of up to €16 000 on the condition that they maintain a traditional menu. Admirable as it may be to support an autochthonic culture, it is difficult to understand why a restaurant that serves bad goulash and is losing its guests should be subsidised with public money, and why innovation and variety are not considered worthy of support. It also ignores the fact that 'traditional' Viennese cuisine is itself a *mélange* of recipes from parts of the former empire. After all, it is more important to try to save the local 'slow food' culture rather than individual items on the menu. Honestly, traditionally heavy Viennese dishes should not be supported but rather banned in the interests of health.

The Beisl is one of the ambiguous symbols of nostalgia in a city where even nostalgia is not what it used to be. It is not solely a comforting and merry place, but also malicious and narrow. This applies to another phenomenon that I sorely miss elsewhere: the Viennese coffee-house. Much has been written about the morphology and the pleasurable aspects of this facility, but little about its typology and effects. Quite different from the Parisian café, it has been a lost-and-sometimes-found office for many years of life and many great products of the mind. It is a place where you can express your annoyance or your satisfaction with anything on earth and always find someone to agree with you. The coffee-house symbolises not merely pleasure, showing-off, distraction, procrastination, inexactitude, slowness and patience – attributes that admittedly make it easier to understand this city – but also a place of fruitful meeting, mediation and *détente* between members and groups of society. During a major annual internet event in the city hall, it is amusing to observe how after a short while most of the data freaks leave the globally connected venue to carry on their discussions in a nearby coffee-house.

Vienna is supposed to be a city of the gourmet,

the epicure and the *bon vivant*. According to an official survey, 56% of its residents do not want to live without good food and drink, whereas holidays (28%), cars (27%) and culture (16%), are also-rans. Human nature being what it is, they reserve the right to pleasure primarily for themselves, and are not so thrilled about others enjoying themselves. This attitude can be seen at best in the battles over the 'Schanigarten' – an extension of a restaurant onto the pavement during fair weather. This practice has existed since 1750, but the Viennese – born saboteur of reality – has not given up his battle against one possibly being set up too close to his flat. Mountains of files in City Hall are witness to the legendary resistance to any new Schanigarten by people who themselves enjoy sitting in them. Since World War II, Vienna has been a city with a disproportionately high number of very old and very cranky women. For decades, the city at night was intended to serve only as a parking lot with a cable TV plug. This anti-social peace of the cemetery once caused a wag to say, "in Vienna, the stage set is beautiful, but the cast needs to be exchanged". Thankfully, this situation has changed. The increasing number of young people who want to use the streets at night, the introduction of global trends of consumption and leisure, political activism against the governing coalition and, above all, travel, have changed the way Viennese use public space. For the first time in history (ignoring for the moment their excursions into neighbouring countries between 1939 and 1945), masses of ordinary Viennese have been able to afford foreign travel. Those who have been to Spain or to Thailand have seen streets used at night by people to meet, drink and eat. Back in Vienna, they suddenly expect to use their city in the same way. The square in front of the imposing City Hall, for instance, has been given over in summer to food stalls offering different cuisines with the backdrop of a huge free open air opera-film theatre – unthinkable a decade ago. Thousands of Italian tourists join the newly outgoing Viennese in the squares at night, a process that has been called the 'Mediterraneanisation' of Vienna.

History is a very subjective field of inquiry, open to manipulation, interpretation and ideological bias. One only has to think of the story of colonialism as seen by the rulers, or the official history of the United States. In Vienna, history has been suppressed and distorted on an unprecedented scale, especially the difficult and embarrassing bits. It is true that, on the surface, it has unparalleled multicultural credentials. Why, this country was even ruled by a foreign dynasty, the Habsburgs, for six hundred years. The dozens of nationalities that fell under the sceptre of Vienna sent their sons and daughters to the capital in droves. The telephone directory is proof of this. There are 21 columns of Novaks (a Czech name) in the Vienna telephone book, while the Prague telephone book shows only 17 columns of Novaks. The typically cynical Viennese would instantly retort, "Not every Novak in Prague has a telephone." The many nationalities, their customs and cuisines that have been present in the city's culture should logically point towards a developed multicultural society. Today, 19% of its residents were born outside the country. Why is it then that a political party with a xenophobic campaign won 27% of the vote in 1999? Something doesn't click here.

Historian Erhard Chvojka has established that the various nationalities that lived here rarely intermingled. There was a highly stratified social system that allocated a different status to each nationality – those of German, Hungarian and Italian origin occupied government posts, Czechs were service providers or workers in brick kilns, Yugoslavs and Poles menial workers and so on. A finely tuned system of racism existed even at a time in history that is idealised as the 'melting pot' period of Austrian culture. This means that at the *fin-de-siècle*, a moment of great attainments in art, music, architecture, literature – dark resentments were brewing between neighbours. One of those unpleasant exports again: both the racism and the strong anti-Semitism obviously made a lasting impression on a certain resident of the city of that time, who went on to plunge the continent into war and genocide.

The varied menus and the many restaurants offering exotic cuisine thus prove nothing other than that Viennese stomachs are not xenophobic. In fact, the presence of several nationalities here is symbolic of a newly international consumer approach to cultures – a pick-and-choose-your-exotic-titbit trend reinforced by television. The Viennese have always assumed that theirs was the best of all possible worlds – apart from its superb cultural quality of life it is one of the rare capitals that has a zero budget deficit – and only those who could provide something they needed were welcome here. They have always tried their best to restrict entry to their dream town, to allow in only those who were good enough for them – legendary composers, architects, *chefs de cuisine* and now computer programmers. 'Compensatory immigration' was desired, to make up for deficits in talent or pension funds, not groups with independent cultural identities or (jesusmariajoseph!) cultural enrichment. In effect, immigrants and their cultures were commercialised and consumerised – other cultures were not respected for what they were but for what they could supply.

Those who have come here have gone about their work regardless, making their respective contributions: the great symphonies, the breathtaking buildings, contemporary dance, DJ-performances, the best coffee outside Italy and the best ice-cream anywhere including Italy. All of which is labelled and consumed as Viennese culture, which is perhaps the best compliment Vienna can pay anyone without really wanting to.

Oh yes, there is one other major export from Vienna that changed the 20th century mind, an invention that, too, was not free of misuse – psychoanalysis. But that would be an entirely new book, and it is now time to stop.

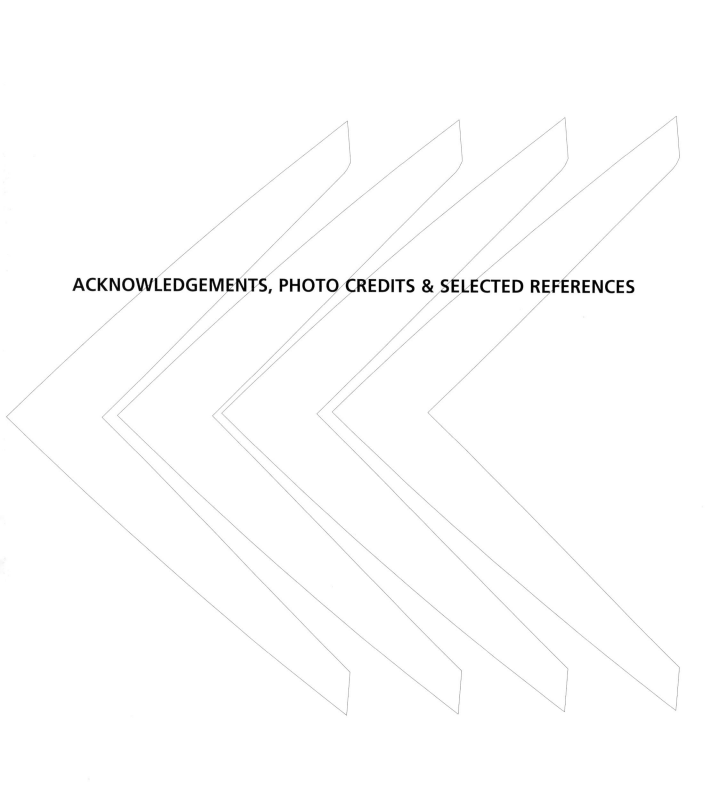

ACKNOWLEDGEMENTS, PHOTO CREDITS & SELECTED REFERENCES

COVER PHOTO: Victoria, Hong Kong; Ramesh K. Biswas, Vienna/Berlin
INSIDE REAR PHOTO: Poor labourer looking at world maps in Bombay; Heinz Nissel, Vienna

A State Of Mind

PHOTOS: **1**: Pudong; **2**: The Bund, Shanghai; **3**: Elevated motorway, Shanghai; Ramesh K. Biswas, Vienna /Berlin

Newman, S.,/Lonsdale, S., Human Jungle. London: BBC/Random House 1996
Calvino, I., La cittá invisibile, Mondadori, 1956

SHANGHAI

PHOTO 1: Pudong; Ramesh K. Biswas, Vienna/Berlin
PHOTO 2: Nanjing Road, Shanghai; Erik-Jan Ouwerkerk, Berlin

Biswas, R.K., An Approach to the Study of Urban Cultures in China. In: Kögel, E./Meyer, U., Ed., The Chinese City. Berlin: Jovis, 2000
Goodman, B., Urban Identity and the Question of a Public Sphere in Chinese Regional Cities. University of California, Berkeley: Center for Chinese Studies Regional Seminar, 1990, Nov. 2 – 3
Howe, C., Shanghai. Revolution and Development in an Asian Metropolis. Cambridge etc.: Cambridge University Press, 1981
Hu X.M./He J., Shanghai banghui jianshi (Short Story of Secret Societies in Shanghai). Shanghai: Renmin Chubanshe, 1991
James, C., Flying Visits (remark about the I-Ching). London: Picador, 1985
Pudong Deptt. of the Chinese Committee for the Support of International Trade, Jinri Pudong (Today's Pudong). Shanghai: 1994
Ma Y.L./Wu D./Gui S.X., Shanghai Pudong xinqu 90 niandai shehui baozhang fazhan guihua yanjiu (Studies for the Development of Social Security in Pudong of the Nineties). Shanghai: Shehuikexueyuan Chubanshe, 1995
Pan, L., Old Shanghai. Gangsters in Paradise. Hong Kong: Heinemann Asia Papers on Shanghai Studies, 1984
Pan, L., Shanghai: A Century of Change. Shanghai yanjiu luncong. Shanghai: Hai Feng Publishing Co., 1995,
Papers on Shanghai Studies. Nr. 1, Nr. 7. Shanghai: Shehuikexueyuan Chubanshe, 1988, 1992
Pilz, E., Shanghai: Die Perle des Ostens. In: Mega-Cities, Brandes & Aspel, 1997
Rehn, D., Shanghais Wirtschaft im Wandel: Mit Spitzentechnologien ins 21. Jahrhundert. Hamburg: Institut für Asienkunde 185, 1990
Schüller, M., Ansturm auf die Städte: Regionalgefälle und Binnenmigration in China. *China aktuell*, June 1995, pp. 494 – 499
Sergeant, H., Shanghai. Collision Point of Cultures 1918/1939. New York: Crown Publishing
Shanghaishi Pudongxinqu guifanxing wenxian huibian (1996): (State and city law in Pudong). Pudong Office for Administration and Legal Matters, 1990
Sit, V.F.S., Chinese Cities. The Growth of the Metropolis since 1949. Oxford/New York/Hong Kong: Oxford University Press, 1985
Wakeman, F. E./Yeh W.S., Shanghai Soujournes. Berkeley: University of California, Institute of East Asian Studies, China Research Monograph 40, 1992
Whyte, M.K., Urban Life in the People's Republic. In: The Cambridge History of China, Bd.15, MacFarquhar R./Fairbank J., Ed., Cambridge: Cambridge University Press, 1991, pp. 682 – 742
Yan, Z.M., Shanghai: The Growth and Shifting Emphasis of China's Largest City. In: Chinese Cities, Victor F.S. Sit, Ed., Oxford/New York/ Hong Kong: Oxford University Press, 1985, pp. 94 – 127
Yao, X.T., Shanghai Xianggang bijiao yanjiu (Vergleichende Studien zu Shanghai und Hong Kong). Shanghai: Renmin Chubanshe, 1990
Yeung, Y.M., Introduction: Urbanization and Development. In: The Urban Transition, Ginsburg, N., Ed., Hong Kong: The Chinese University Press XI – XVI, 1990a
Yeung, Y.M./Sung, Y.W., Shanghai: Transformation and Modernization under China's Open Policy. Hong Kong: The Chinese University Press, 1996
Yeung Y.M./ Hu X.W., Chinese Coastal Cities. Catalysts for Modernization. Honolulu: University of Hawai Press, 1992
Zhang, Z., Jindai Shanghai chengshi yanjiu (Modern Shanghai). Shanghai: Renmin Chubanshe, 1990
Zhang, Z./ Xiong, Y.Z./ Pan, J.X./ Song, Y.L., Jindai Shanghai chengshi de fazhan, tedian he yanjiu lilun (Modern Shanghai). *Jindaishi yanjiu* 1991/4, pp. 19 – 38
Zheng, Z., "Pudong" lishi fazhan gaishuo. In: Shanghaishi yanjiu Bd.2 (Shanghai Studies), Tang Z.C./Shen H.C., Ed., Shanghai: Xuelin Chubanshe, 1988, pp. 397 – 406

TOKYO

PHOTO 1: Shinjiku; Ramesh K. Biswas, Vienna/Berlin
PHOTO 2: Pachinko parlour purgatory, Shinjiku; Ramesh K. Biswas, Vienna/Berlin

Bestor, T.C., Neighborhood Tokyo. Stanford: Stanford University Press, 1989
Bestor, T.C., ., Tōkyō no Daidokoro: Research on the Tsukiji Wholesale Fish Market *Japan Foundation Newsletter*, 17, no.4,1989, pp. 17 – 21
Clammer, J., Contemporary Urban Japan: A Sociology of Consumption. Oxford: Blackwell, 1997
Fowler, E., San'ya Blues: Laboring Life in Contemporary Tokyo. Ithaca and London: Cornell University Press, 1996
Guzewicz, T. D., A New Generation of Homeless. *Japan Quarterly* 43,3, 1996, pp. 43 – 53
Hadfield, P., Sixty Seconds that Will Change the World: The Coming Tokyo Earthquake. London: Pan Books, 1992
Jinnai, H., Tokyo: A Spatial Anthropology. Translated by K. Nishimura, Berkeley and Los Angeles: University of California Press,   1995
Lewis, M., How a Tokyo Earthquake Could Devastate Wall Street and the World Economy. *Manhattan, Inc.*, June 1989, pp. 69 – 79

Ministry of Justice, Statistics Department, Government of Japan

Popham, P., Tokyo: The City at the End of the World. Tokyo: Kodansha International, 1985

Sassen, S., The Global City: New York, London, Tokyo. Princeton: Princeton University Press, 1991

Seidensticker, E., Low City, High City: Tokyo from Edo to the Earthquake. Rutland, Vt. and Tokyo: Charles E. Tuttle, 1983

Seidensticker, E., Tokyo Rising: The City since the Great Earthquake. New York: Alfred A. Knopf, 1990

Waley, P., Tokyo Now and Then: An Explorer's Guide. New York and Tokyo: Weatherhill, 1984

Wurman, R. S., Tokyo Access. New York: Access Press, 1984

Home page: www.jinjapan.org/

BOMBAY

PHOTO 1: Poor man feeding birds; Henning Stegmüller, Munich

PHOTO 2: Bazaar; Anirban Banerjee, Vienna

Banerjee-Ghua, S., Urban Development Process in Bombay: Planning for Whom?. In: Patel/Thorner, 1996c, pp. 100 – 200

Biswas, R.K., Das Geld liegt auf dem Lebensweg. Stadtbauwelt, 140, 29. Dez., 1998, pp. 2606 – 2613

Biswas, R.K., Urban Architectures in India. In: Biswas, R.K., Magical Hands. Vienna: 1993

Biswas, R.K., Urban Transformations. Architecture+Design, New Delhi, 1992

Bronger, D., Die Rolle der Megastadt im Entwicklungsprozess – Das Beispiel Bombay.
  In: Megastädte, Feldbauer P./Rünzler D./Pilz E./Stacher I., Ed., Wien/Köln/Weimar: Böhlau, 1993, pp. 107 – 128

Chakravorty, S., Too Little, in the Wrong Places? Mega City Programme: Efficiency and Equity in Indian Urbanisation. In: *Economic & Political Weekly*, September 1996, pp. 2565 – 2572

Country Study India. World Bank, Washington: 1999

Engineer, Ashgar A., Lifting the Veil: Communal Violence and Harmony in Contemporary India. Hyderabad: Sangam Books, 1995

Harris, N., Bombay in a Global Economy. Cities, 12/3, 1995, pp. 175 – 184

Joshi, V./Little, I.M.B., Indian`s Economic Reforms 1991 – 2000. Oxford: Clarendon Press, 1996

Lele, J., Saffronization of the Shiv Sena: The Political Economy of City, State and Nation. In: Pathel S./Thorner A. 1996

Mehrota, R., Bombay. Bombay: 1998

Mehrota, R., Ein Ort, Zwei Welten. *Stadtbauwelt*, 140, 29. Dez. 1998, pp. 2614 – 2620

Murphey, R., The Outsiders: The Western Experience in India and China. Ann Arbor: University of Michigan Press, 1977

Nest, G., Bombay first?. *Stadtbauwelt*, 140, 29. Dez. 1998, pp. 2604 – 2606

Nest, G., Kamathipura, Red Light District. *Stadtbauwelt*, 140, 29. Dez. 1998, pp. 2656 – 2658

Nissel, H., Megastadt Bombay – Global City Mumbai?. Mega-Cities, Brandes & Aspel, 1997

Nissel, H., Bombay in Zeiten der Globalisierung. *Stadtbauwelt*, 140, 29. Dez. 1998, pp. 2620 – 2630

Panwalkar P., Slum-Ökonomie in Dharavi. *Stadtbauwelt*, 140, 29. Dez. 1998, pp. 2640 – 2646

Panwalkar, P., Upgradation of Slums: A World Bank Programme. In: Pathel S./Thorner A. 1996, pp. 121 – 142

Patel, S./Thorner, A., 2 Volumes, Bombay. Metaphor for Modern India. Bombay: Oxford University Press, 1996, and Bombay.

Mosaic of Modern Culture. Bombay: Oxford University Press, 1996

Tindall, G., City of Gold. Biography of Bombay. London: In: Patel S./Thorner A., 1982, pp. 64 – 85

LONDON

PHOTO 1: Millennium Bridge; Foster Associates, London

PHOTO 2: Soho; Ramesh K. Biswas, Vienna/Berlin

Castells, M./Hall, P., Technopoles of the World. London and New York: Routledge: 1994

Knox, P./Taylor, P.S., World Cities in a World System. Cambridge, GB: Cambridge University Press, 1995

Fletcher, G., The London nobody knows. London: Ward lock, 1996

Inwood, St., A History of London. London: Macmillan, 2000

Kennedy, R., London: World city moving into the 21st century. London: The Stationary Office Books, 1991

Matsan, M., Modernising Britain: the last rotten borough. Fabian Society, 1997

Powell, K., London. London: Academy Editions, 1993

Home page: www.london.gov.uk

HONG KONG

PHOTO 1: Road directions in Victoria; Ramesh K. Biswas, Vienna/Berlin

PHOTO 2: Panorama of Hong Kong; Information Services Department, Govt. of Hong Kong SAR

Castells, M./Goh, L./Yingwang Kwok, R., The Shek Kip Mei Syndrome: Economic Development and Public Housing in Hong Kong and Singapore. 1990

Cheng T.Y./Lin T.B./Kuan H.C., Economic and Public Affairs for Hong Kong. Hong Kong: Far East Publications, 1979

Cuthbert, A.R., The Alienation of Public Space in Hong Kong. Public Spaces in Asia-Pacific Cities, Piu Miao, Ed., Manoa: University of Hawaii Press, 1999

Cuthbert, A.R., The Genesis of Land Use Planning and Urban Development. Land Use Transport Planning in Hong Kong. The End of an Era Ch2, Dimitriou, H.T./Cook, A.S., Ed., Ashgate London: 1998, pp. 35 – 54

Cuthbert, A.R., Density and Urban Structures. Proceedings of The 3rd Int. Conference on Tall Buildings, Cheung,C.K. and Lee, P.K.K., Ch 18,

1984, pp. 410 – 415

Cuthbert, A.R., Ambiguous Space, Ambiguous Rights - Corporate Power and Social Control in Hong Kong (with K. McKinnell), Cities, Vol 14, no 51997, pp. 295 – 311

Cuthbert, A.R., The Right to the City: Surveillance, Private Interest and the Public Domain in Hong Kong. *Cities*, Vol 12, no 5, Oct 1995, pp. 293 – 310

Cuthbert, A.R., For a Few Dollars More: Urban Planning and the Legitimation Process in Hong Kong. *The International Journal of Urban and Regional Research,* Vol 15, No 4, 1992

Cuthbert A.R, Hong Kong. Unpublished PhD.Thesis, London School of Economics, 1988 Government Information Services, Hong Kong Background Facts, HK: Govt. of Hong Kong SAR, 1999

Hayes, J., Hong Kong: Tale of Two Cities. In: Majorie Topley (ed.), Hong Kong: The Interaction of Tradition and Live in the Towns. Hong Kong: Hong Kong Branch of the Royal Asiatic Society, 1975, pp. 1 – 10

Henderson, J., Danger and Opportunity in the Asia-Pacific. In: Grahame Thompson (ed.), Economic Dynamism in the Asia-Pacific. London: Routledge, 1998

Henderson, J., Urbanisation in the Hong Kong-South China Region: An Introduction to Dynamics and Dilemmas. *International Journal of Urban and Regional Research*, 15(2), 1991

Hong Kong Trade Development Council, Hong Kong Economy Profile. 1999, Government Information Services, Hong Kong Background Facts, HK: Govt. of Hong Kong SAR, 1999

Jarvie, I. C., Window on Hong Kong: A Sociological Study of the Hong Kong Film Industry and Its Audience. Hong Kong: Centre of Asian Studies, University of Hong Kong, 1977 Kan A.W.S., A Study of Neighborly Interaction in Public Housing: The Case of Hong Kong. Hong Kong: The Chinese University of Hong Kong, 1974

Lang, O., Chinese Family and Society. New Haven: Yale University Press, 1946

Lau, S.K., Society and Politics in Hong Kong. The Chinese University Press, 1984

Lee, R. P. L., Corruption in Hong Kong: Congruence of Chinese Social Norms with Legal Norms. Unpublished paper, 1977

Lee, R. P. L., Cheung Tak-sing and Cheung Yuet-wah, Material and Non-material Conditions and Life Satisfaction of Urban Residents in Hong Kong. In: Tzong-biau Lin T.B./Rance P.L. Lee/Simonis U.E., Ed., Hong Kong: Economic, Social and Political Studies in Development. White Plains: M. E. Sharpe, Inc., 1979, pp. 83 – 94

Liu, W.T., Family interaction Among Local and Refugee Chinese Families in Hong Kong. *Journal of Marriage and Family* 28, 3 (August), 1966, pp. 314 – 323

Morris, J., Hong Kong: Epilogue to an Empire. Penguin Books, 1988

Miners, N.J., The Government and Politics of Hong Kong. Hong Kong: Oxford University Press, 1977

Mitchell, R.E., Levels of Emotional Strain in Southeast Asian Cities. 2 volumes. Hong Kong: A Project of the Urban Family Life Survey, 1969a

Michell, R.E., Family Life in Urban Hong Kong. 2 volumes. Hong Kong: Project Report of the Urban Family Life Survey, 1969b

Schiffer, J., The Hong Kong Model. 1983

Walden, J., Who`s Who in Hong Kong. Hong Kong: South China Morning Post, 2000

Wong F.M., Modern Ideology, Industrialization, and Conjugalism: The Hong Kong case. *International Journal of Sociology of Family 2*, 2 (September), 1972, pp. 139 – 150

Wong F.M., Industrialization and Family Structure in Hong Kong. *Journal of Marriage and the Family* 37, 4 Nov., 1975, pp. 958 – 1000

LAS VEGAS

PHOTO 1: The Strip at night; Las Vegas News Bureau

PHOTO 2: Show girls; Las Vegas News Bureau

Banham, R., Los Angeles Times West Magazine, November 8, 1970

Berns, D., Venice in Las Vegas. *Las Vegas Review-Journal*, 27

Daniel, P., Say It With Flowers. Hotel Bellagio, Blueprint, 12, 1998

Hess, H., Las Vegas NY-NY Casino-Hotel Shows How to Keep the Crowds Coming. *Architectural Record*, 3, 1997

Hitchcock, H.-R., An Eastern Critic Looks at Western Architecture. *California Arts and Architecture*, December 1940 King, S., The Stand. 1992

Rothman, H., Ed., Reopening the American West. Tucson: University of Arizona Press, 1997

Venturi, R./Scott Brown, D./Izenour, S., Learning From Las Vegas. Cambridge: MIT Press, 1972

Whyte, W., In Fortune Magazine, 1958

Wolfe, T., The Kandy-Kolored Tangerine-Flake Streamline Baby. New York: Farrar, Straus & Giroux, 1965

MARSEILLE

PHOTO 1: Street scene; Suzanna Lauterbach, Berlin

PHOTO 2: Sailors in the port area; Anna Blau, Vienna

Boura, O., Marseille ou la mauvaise reputation. Paris: Gallimard, 1997

Izzo, J.C., Total Chéops. Paris: Gallimard, 1995

Medam, A., 'Marseille Blues', Stadtbauwelt, 138, 26. Juni 1998, pp. 1366 – 1374

Peraldi, M., Entre logeurs et logés: l'épreuve territoriale. Edition Cerfise, Marseille 1989

Peraldi, M., Paysage, ville et mémoire Marseille. Edition Cerfise, Marseille 1998

Peraldi, M., Les noms du social dans l'urbain en crise. Edition Cerfise, Marseille 1988

KUALA LUMPUR

PHOTO 1: Chinatown with five-foot-ways; Ramesh K. Biswas, Vienna/Berlin
PHOTO 2: View from the top of the Twin Towers during construction; Ramesh K. Biswas, Vienna/Berlin

Biswas, R.K., Kuala Lumpur. *Domus*, 808, Milano: Oct. 1998, pp. 10 – 12
Biswas, R.K., Von der Zinnsuche zur Sinnsuche. *Stadtbauwelt*, 132, 27. Dez. 1996, pp. 2712 – 2721
Burgess, A., The Malayan Trilogy. London: Penguin Books
Chen, V.F., Encyclopaedia of Malaysia, Architecture Volume, 1999
Lat, Town Boy. Kuala Lumpur: Straits Times Publishing Co., 1999
Lim, J.C.S., Die Eroberung des Dschungels oder der Sieg der Vernunft. *Stadtbauwelt*, 132, 27. Dez. 1996, pp. 2732 – 2738
Lim, T.N., Eine asiatische Stadt im Wandel. *Stadtbauwelt*, 132, 27.Dez. 1996, pp. 2740 – 2744
Heng, J.S., Vom Shophouse zur Megamall – der Verfall des öffentlichen Raums. *Stadtbauwelt*, 132, 27.Dez. 1996, pp. 2722 – 2726
Mahathir, M., The Malay Dilemma. 1970
Turnbull, C. M., A Short History of Malaysia, Singapore & Brunei. Sydney: Cassell 1980
Winstedt, R., A History of Malaya. London: Porcupine Press, 1979
Home pages: http://mcsl.mampu.gov.my/; http://www.mdc.com; http://www.kempen.gov.my/

ISTANBUL

PHOTO 1: View of Istanbul over the Bosphorus from building site; Nelly Rau-Hering, Berlin
PHOTO 2: Modern woman passes building workers at prayer; Nelly Rau-Hering, Berlin

Celik, C., The Remaking of Istanbul. Berkley: University of California Press, 1993
Eldem, E./Goffmann, D./Masters, B.A., Ottoman City Between East and West: Aleppo, Izmir, and Istanbul. Cambridge: Cambridge University Press, 2000
Freely, J., Istanbul: The Imperial City. Penguin Books, 1998
Froschauer, E.-M./Volker M., Tausend Häuser in einer Nacht. *Stadtbauwelt*, 135, 25. Sept. 1998, pp. 2022 – 2028
Onay, Y., Zivile Stadtgesellschaft oder fundamentalistische Ordnung. Stadtbauwelt, 135, 25. Sept. 1998, pp. 2010 – 2011
Yerasimos, S., Wie groß ist Istanbul?. *Stadtbauwelt*, 135, 25. Sept. 1998, pp. 2012 – 2018

SOWETO

PHOTO 1: Aerial view of Soweto; Henning Rasmuss, Johannesburg
PHOTO 2: Church meeting in Soweto with Jo'burg in background; Henning Rasmuss, Johannesburg

African National Congress, The Reconstruction and Development Programme. Johannesburg: Umanyano Publications, 1994
Armour, J., Your South African Home. Cape Town: Howard Timmins, 1964, p.52, ISF Working Group, GAPS Architects and Urban Planners. 1993
Bremner, L., Crime and the Emerging Landscape of Post-apartheid Johannesburg. In: blank_
Carter, G.M., The Politics of Inequality. London: Thames and Hudson, 1958
Central Archives, Draft Memorandum on the Group of Areas Bill. 1950
Central Archives, Eviction Notice. Native Affairs Department, NTS 5314/77/313(E)
Chipkin, C., Johannesburg Syle: Architecture & Society 1880´s – 1960´s. 1993
Chipkin, C., Preparing for Apartheid. Essay, 1993
Coetzee, J.M., White Writing. New Haven: Yale University-Press, 1988
Crankshaw, O., Race, Class and the Changing Division of Labour under Apartheid. 1997
Dewar, D., South African Cities: A Manifesto for Change. 1991
Dörning, Maj, W., Lessons of the Past in Dealing with the Terrorist Threat. Paratus, September 1983 Hahn, T., Report and Proceedings with Appendices of the Government Commission on Native Laws and Customs. 1883
Hallen, H., Buildings Stand Still, People Move. *KZ-NIA Journal*, 1997
Judin, H./Vladislavic, I., blank_ Architecture, Apartheid and After. Rotterdam: NAI Publishers, 1998
Knox, P./Gutsche, P., Do you Know Johannesburg?. Vereeniging: Unie-Volkspeers, 1947, p. 15
Kuzawayo, E., Call Me Woman. Johannesburg: Ravan Press, 1958
Minkley, G., Border Dialogues: Space and the Industrialization of East London.
Mlangeni, B., Matchbox Homes und Township Villas. *Stadtbauwelt*, 133, 27. März 1997, pp. 622 – 630
Ndebele, N., Fools and Other Stories. 1983
Platzky,L./Walker, C., The Surplus People: Forced Removals in South Africa. Johannesburg: Ravan Press, 1995
Posel, D., The Making of Apartheid 1948 – 1961. 1991
Posel, D., Apatheid´s Genesis. 1994
Report of the Committee for the Constitutional Affairs of the President`s Council on an Urbanization Strategy of the Republic of Southf Africa. Pretoria: Government Printers, 1985
Rich, P., A Hybrid Architecture Takes Root. Architecture SA, May/June, 1986
Robinson, J., The Power of Apartheid. 1996
Silvermann, M., Provincial Government White Paper on Urban Regeneration for Gauteng. 1997
Silvermann, M., Eastern Sector Development Strategy for the Johannesburg Metropolitan Council. 1995
Swilling, M., Governing Africa's Cities. 1996
Verwoerd, H.F., Apartheid. London: Routledge and Kegan Paul, 1968

BERLIN

PHOTO 1: Info-Box on Potsdamer Platz; Anna Blau, Vienna
PHOTO 2: Potsdamer Platz at night; Erik-Jan Ouwerkerk, Berlin

Biswas, R.K., Die Erlaubte Stadt. *Bauwelt*, 42, 6. Nov. 1998, pp. 2370 – 2372
Cullen, M., Der Reichstag. Parlament, Denkmal, Symbol. Berlin: 1995
Düttmann, M./Zwoch, F., Bauwelt Berlin Annual: Chronik der baulichen Ereignisse 1996 bis 2000. 4 volumes, Berlin: Birkhäuser 1996, 1997, 1998, 1999/2000
Fuchs, G./Moltmann, B./Prigge, W., Ed., Mythos Metropole. Frankfurt a.M.: Suhrkamp, 1995
Hoffmann-Axthelm, D., Neues Herz oder neue Insel. *Bauwelt*, 42, 6. Nov. 1998, pp.2356 – 2366
Hoidn, B./Jakubeit, B. Ed., Schloss – Palast – Haus. Basel/Berlin/Boston: Birkhäuser 1998
Hotzan, J., dtv-Atlas zur Stadt: Von den ersten Gründungen bis zur modernen Stadtplanung. dtv, 1994
Koolhaas, R., Stadtkultur an der Jahrtausendwende. In: Kursbuch Stadt, Stadtleben und Stadtkultur an der Jahrtausendwende. Stuttgart: 1999
Lampugnani, V. M./Mönninger, M., Ed., Berlin Morgen. Stuttgart: 1991
Meyer, U., Ed., Capital City Berlin. Berlin: Jovis, 1999
Pobach, M., Weltstadt. Architektur und Städtebau am Potsdamer Platz, Berlin: 1998
Senatsverwaltung für Bau- und Wohnungswesen, Ed., Projekte für die Hauptstadt Berlin. Städtebau und Architektur, Bericht 34, 1996
Stimmann, H. Ed., Physiognomy of a Metropolis. Skira: Milano 2000
Stimmann, H., Berliner Abkommen. *Bauwelt*, 89. Jg., 1998
Stimmann, H., Ed., Zwoch, F., Berlin, Babylon etc. Basel/Berlin/Boston: Birkhäuser 1995
Wefing, H., Berlin. In: Kursbuch Stadt. Stuttgart: 1999
Wise, M., Capital Dilemma. Germany's Search for a New Architecture of Democracy. New York: 1998
Zohlen, G., Berlin – Offene Stadt. Die Erneuerung seit 1989. Berlin: 1999
Zwoch, F., Ed., Hauptstadt Berlin, Parlamentsviertel, Spreebogen. Basel/Berlin/Boston: Birkhäuser 1993
Zwoch, F., Ed., Hauptstadt Berlin, Spreeinsel. Basel/Berlin/Boston: Birkhäuser 1995

SÃO PAULO

PHOTO 1: Avenida Paulista, São Paulo; Anirban Banerjee, Vienna
PHOTO 2: Electioneering on the avenida Paulista, São Paulo; Andreas Novy, Vienna

Adorno, S., Gestão Filantrópica da Probe za Urbana São Paulo em Perspectiva 4. São Paulo: SEADE, 1990, pp. 9 – 17
Barelli, W./Dedecca/Salvadori, C., Análise do comportamento dos salários e da massa salarial na Grande São Paulo. In: SEADE, Mercado de tra balho na Grande São Paulo, 1989
Wilson, C., Auge e Inflexão da Desconcentração Economica Regional. São Paulo: Affonso, Silva, 1995
Feagin, J.R./Smith, M.P., Cities and the New International Division of Labour: An Overview. In: The Capitalist City: Global Restructuring and Community Politics. Feagin, J.R./Smith, M.P., Ed., Oxford New York: 1987
Feldbauer P./Gächter A./Hardach, G./Novy, A., Ed., Frankfurt a. M./Wien: 1995 Novy, A., Soziale Bewegung und Stadtplanung in São Paulo (1920 – 1980). *Zeitschrift für Lateinamerika* 48: Planer und Bürger, 1995, pp. 25 – 44
Novy, A., São Paolo: Metropole Südamerikas. Mega-Cities, Brandes & Aspel, 1997
Novy, A./Calzadilla, B., Die Industrialisierung Brasiliens. In: Industrialisierung. Enwicklungsprozesse,
Rolnik, R. et al, São Paulo: Crise e Mudanca. São Paulo: Brasiliense, 1990

MOSCOW

PHOTO 1: Models resting in lift between photo sessions; Olaf Martens, Leipzig
PHOTO 2: Moscow street scene with young woman and *babushka*; Olaf Martens, Leipzig

Akademija Stroitelstwo i Architekturi SSSR/Architekturno-Planirowotschnoje Uprawneije G. Mokswij/Sojus Architekturno-SSSR: Planirowka i Sastroika Moskwa 1945 – 1957
Baranow, N.N., Die Silhouette der Stadt. Leningrad: 1980
Dachno, W.P., Massenwohnbau in der UdSSR. *Der Architekt*, 2/1994
Frauendorfer, H., Moskau, Oktober 1998. *Stadtbauwelt*, 141, 26. März 1999, pp. 634 – 638
Godleevskij, Stadtbaukunst des Mittelalters, in Dolgner D./Roch I., Berlin: 1990
Goldhoorn, B., Wilder Osten – Western Standard. *Stadtbauwelt*, 141, 26. März 1999, pp. 630 – 634
Hain, S., Reise nach Moskau. Wie Deutsche "sozialistisch" bauen lernten. *Bauwelt* 45, 1992
Hoffmann-Axthelm, D., Moskauer Stadtstruktur: Die Übermacht der Bilder. *Stadtbauwelt*, 141, 26. März 1999, pp. 646 – 660
Malfroy, S./Zierau, F., Tabula rasa de facto. Werk/Bauen + Wohnen 12, 1999
Margolina, S., Moskau, fremde Metropole. Stadtbauwelt, 141, 26. März 1999, pp. 610 – 620
Kopp, A., Town and Revolution. Soviet Architecture and City Planning 1917 – 1935, London: 1973
Kostock, V.V., Enwicklung der Gestaltung russischer Stadtfestungen des Mittelalters. In: N.N.
Pamjatnik, Architeknurni Moskwi. Bd 5, Semlaja Gorod, Moskau: 1989
Schlögel, K., Moskau lesen. Berlin: Siedler, 1984
Sinik, S., Horror Novel of Emigration. London 1989

SINGAPORE

PHOTO 1: Panorama; Singapore Tourist Authority
PHOTO 2: Multicultural; Singapore Tourist Authority

Barber N., Sinister Twilight – The Fall of Singapore.
Collins, R., Raffles, a biography.
Edwards, N./Keys, P., Singapore: a Guide to Buildings, Streets Places.
Josey, A., Singapore: Its Past, Present and Future.
Josey, A., Lee Kuan Yew – The Struggle for Singapore.
Sesser, S., The Lands of Charm and Cruelty. London: Picador, 1994
Turnball, C. M., A History of Singapore. Sydney: Cassell 1980
Vasil, R., Governing Singapore.
Far Eastern Economic Review, several articles
Asiaweek, several articles
Home page: http://www.gov.sg/

VIENNA

PHOTO 1: Food stalls & free opera theatre in front of City Hall; Ramesh K. Biswas, Vienna/Berlin
PHOTO 2: Naschmarkt (Main food market) Ramesh K. Biswas, Vienna/Berlin

Andics, H., Die Insel der Seligen. München: Wilhelm Goldmann, 1968
Anwander,B., Beiseln und Altwiener Gaststätten. Wien: Falter, 1991
Banik-Schweitzer, R./Lachnit, P./Ehalt, H. C., Etc., Wien wirklich. Wien: Verlag für Gesellschaftskritik, 1983
Biswas, R.K., A Certain Lack of Respect. In: M1:333. Biswas, R.K., New York: Springer, 1996
Biswas, R.K., Wien, wie es isst. *Stadtbauwelt*, 126, 30. Juni 1995, pp. 1338 – 1342
Ehalt, H. C., Wiener Beisln. Wien: Jugend & Volk, 1985
Fassmann, H./Münz, R., Einwanderungsland Österreich?. Wien: Jugend & Volk, 1995
Grieser, D., Wien. München/Berlin: Amalthea, 1994
Heindl, G., Wo selbst die Engel Urlaub machen. Wien: Paul Neff, 1972
Heindl, G., Wien. Wien/Berlin: Paul Neff, 1972
Kraus, K., Die letzten Tage der Menschheit. Frankfurt a.M.: Suhrkamp, 1986
Maimann, H./Mattl, S., Die Kälte des Februar. Wien: Junius, 1984
Maimann, H./Stadler, K.R./Mattl, S., Mit uns zieht die neue Zeit. Wien: Habarta & Habarta, 1981
Mattl, S., The Streets of Vienna. In: M1:333. Biswas, R.K., New York: Springer, 1996
Mattl, S., The 20th Century. History of Vienna. Volume 6; Vienna: Pichler 2000
Pohanka, R., Das alte Wien. Wien: Jugend & Volk, 1993
Ponger, L., Fremdes Wien. Klagenfurt/Celovec – Salzburg/Wien: Wieser, 1993
Pruckner, H./Weisch, W., Schmelztiegel Wien – einst und jetzt. Wien/Köln: Böhlau, 1990
Steidl, N., Wien. München: Martin Velbinger, 1982
Vergo, P., Vienna 1900. Edinburgh: Her Majesty's Stationery Office, 1983
Zweig S., Stadt der Geniesser
Home page: http://www.magwien.gv.at

ACKNOWLEDGEMENTS

My gratitude to

three close friends: Felix Zwoch, Editor of the StadtBauwelt, for our fruitful cooperation over the years, for his advice, generosity and hilarious sarcasm; Siegfried Mattl, Professor of Contemporary History at the University of Vienna, for his discerning opinions and encyclopaedic knowledge; and Alexander Cuthbert, Professor and Head of Town Planning at the University of New South Wales, Sydney, for his constant encouragement and merciless criticism;

my co-authors for their cooperation and tolerance of my rather radical editing; the photographers and translators; my publishers for their unmitigated support, especially Rudolf Siegle, head of Springer, also Angela Fössl, Frank Christian May, David Marold and Edwin Schwarz; Kerstin Wieland, Peter Strumpf and everyone else at the Bauwelt in Berlin; and of course, Al Gore for inventing the Internet.

Acknowledgements to Stan Sesser and Alfred Knopf Inc. (Random House) for permission to quote; and to Bertelsmann Fachzeitschriften GmbH. I have no sponsors to thank – in the interests of independence, no direct or indirect sponsorship or hospitality offered by any of the cities was accepted.

I can name only very few of the hundreds of people with whom I have had fruitful discussions about cities: Zhou Yun-Bin, Anirban Banerjee, Sandeep Chawla, Victor Chin, Erhard Chvojka, Hubert C. Ehalt, Eva-Maria Froschauer, Mehru & Asif Hasnain, Jeffrey Henderson, Hou Han Rou, Rem Koolhaas, Wolfgang Kos, Kengo Kuma, Desmond Lam, Jimmy Lim, Lim Teng Ngiom, Christine Lixl, Völker Martin, Rahul Mehrotra, James Muldoon, Franz Nahrada, Heinz Nissel, Hans Ulrich Obrist, Herwig Palme, Erich Pilz, Richard Rogers, Reeta Roy, T. Sasitharan, Dietmar Steiner, Akira Suzuki, Wu Jiang.

Finally I would like to thank those who helped in my own office in different ways with the production of the book: Beatrix Bakondy, Nita Tandon, Alexandra Millonig, Daniel Bednarzek, Margarete Endl, Margit Biswas-Brenner and the others.

I dedicate this book to my lovely little son Kenzo, an enthusiastic traveller and lover of cities.